GENTLEMEN CRICKETERS OF MALDON

GENTLEMEN CRICKETERS OF MALDON

Two Hundred and Fifty Years of Cricket in an Essex Town

Richard Cooper

Oxford Publishing Services
Oxford

Published in 2005 by Oxford Publishing Services
34 Warnborough Road
Oxford OX2 6JA

ISBN 0-9550031-0-5

Typeset in Berkeley Oldstyle by Oxford Publishing Services, Oxford
Graphics by Mick Martin
Cover by Andrew Meaden
Printed by Antony Rowe Limited

Contents

List of Illustrations

Images appear by kind permission of the following: Maldon Society, 1, 5, 7, 15, 17; Sussex Record Office, 9 (PH. 6356); Nottinghamshire County Cricket Club, 10; Mrs W. Chick, 16; Mr L. Hardy-King, 18, 19; Mr G. Newman, 21, 23–30; remaining items from the personal collections of the author and others.

Acknowledgements

Thank you to the many people who have assisted in the production of this book. My son, Thomas, mastered the microfilm equipment at the Essex Record Office and spent many hours lost in newspapers of two centuries ago. The people there and at Colchester and Chelmsford libraries were always helpful.

Drs Arthur Brown and Bill Petchey of Essex University fired my enthusiasm for local history and I have delved into David Hughes's enjoyable book, *The Maldonians* for a flavour of Maldon at the end of the nineteenth century. Ken Stubbings's *Here's Good Luck to the Pint Pot* gave me a lot of information about the town's inns, taverns and alehouses. Thanks to Shepherd Neame Ltd for their help with the set-up costs.

Michael Dowsett, author of *The Day of 'The Demon'*, has helped with the account of the matches against C. I. Thornton's XI, and with his own recollections of cricket at Maldon. Many others have been generous with their time and memories, notably Dennis Fenn, Tony Gower, Tom Gozzett, Laurie Hardy-King, Geoff Newman and Claud Rayner, who have helped to shape Part 5 of the book.

Graham Warwick and John Pakey, successive sports editors of the *Maldon & Burnham Standard*, readily found space in their busy pages to publish the short articles on which the book is based.

Michael Martin is responsible for the book's graphics but, more than that, he and his colleague, Lester Crook, have given invaluable support over the final stages of publication. Finally, thanks to my family for the understanding, privacy and funds that were necessary to transform my folly into a tangible work of history.

Introduction: Maldon in 1755

Imagine a town on a hill that is home to one thousand people, the wealthiest of whom have settled into big houses at the top of the High Street. Outside their houses, the street market bulges with produce from surrounding farms where booming agriculture makes rich men of landowners and tenants. The taverns are bursting with dealers and drinkers while visitors take rooms at the smart hotels. The town is a fashionable centre, a place of culture and entertainment, and a seaside resort.

Down the hill, the real source of the town's wealth flows. Homes for the majority of the townsfolk have sprung up on the river bank where they labour ceaselessly on the wharves. Their little pleasure comes from clusters of alehouses, where womenfolk make up the household income when sailors are in port. The port is one of the most important in southeast England, shipping goods from Essex and Hertfordshire to London and the continent. The economy of Chelmsford, the capital town of Essex, is entirely landlocked.

Having grown rich from river trade and dock labour, the merchant families set about the business of social improvement. Soon gentlemen of Maldon are visiting London, spending time in coffee houses, clubs and assembly rooms that are the weave of the capital's social fabric. The thrice-weekly stagecoach between the Aldgate Bull and the Maldon King's Head becomes ever busier as London families come as guests to Maldon's fashionable houses.

And the craze among the aspirant society is cricket. Long had peasant and labourer played the makeshift game, but its

1. The tide swells the river at Potman Marsh. The river Chelmer at Fullbridge with All Saints' and St Peter's towers against the sky.

adoption by the aristocracy has made it the manly and dignified pursuit of Georgian gentlemen. By the 1730s, Frederick Prince of Wales, heir to George II, was patron of games at Moulsey Hurst (near Hampton Court) and great matches were commonplace at London grounds, including the legendary artillery ground at Moorgate and Mr Smith's Pied Horse in Chiswell Street.

Although too parsimonious to risk the enormous sums gambled on matches by their noblemen role models, Maldon's men of business can only stake their claim to social acceptance by bringing home the game of cricket. At the bottom of Market Hill, where effluent flows from the big houses into the estuary, and alehouses snuggle around the Fullbridge wharves, lie the open expanses of Potman Marsh. Here the annual September horse races are held and town fairs and celebrations are centred. Mr Talladay at the White Hart – when he is not promoting bull baiting – sells grazing rights and reaps good profits from the many visitors to events on the marsh.

Potman Marsh, protected for centuries by low seawalls because of the military value of The Causeway, is the natural place for the gentlemen of Maldon to test their skills with bat, ball and wickets. It is natural too for them to resort to the Ship tavern across the Fullbridge, where a gentleman's every pleasure can be supplied.

Part 1

The Years on Potman Marsh

Chapter 1

The challenges of 1755

By 1755 the ancient parish of All Saints, Maldon, had become the fashionable place for wealthy merchants to live. Opposite the distinctive triangular steeple of the church, the King's Head lay at the heart of local affairs, providing both social and commercial resort for men of trade. In the High Street, the market flourished and the London flyer brought well-to-do visitors to the inn. In back room bars, farmers and dealers sealed their business with port and tobacco while public meetings and auctions proceeded in the large front rooms.

The King's Head was owned by Joseph Pattison, a merchant who had once been apprentice master to Maldon's legendary 42-stone fat man, Edward Bright (1721–50). His tenant, Thomas Brand, ran the inn and took profits from its many activities, but, in 1755, he took an ill-advised decision to venture into the growing business of cricket promotion.

From the early years of the eighteenth century cricket had become the craze of the aristocracy. The game required sporting dexterity that was considered both manly and dignified and its complexities offered limitless opportunities for gambling. By 1740 it was commonplace for publicans, given a wealthy backer and a piece of green, to promote cricket matches and take the profits from the food and drink supplied to the teams and their guests. Money matches could also attract large crowds of spectators demanding refreshments from the landlord's tents on the ground. With an eye to such profits, Thomas Brand issued a challenge on behalf of Maldon Cricket Club to play against any other town in Essex.

The challenge appeared in the *Ipswich Journal*, the newspaper covering the Essex area, on 5 July 1755 and set a stake

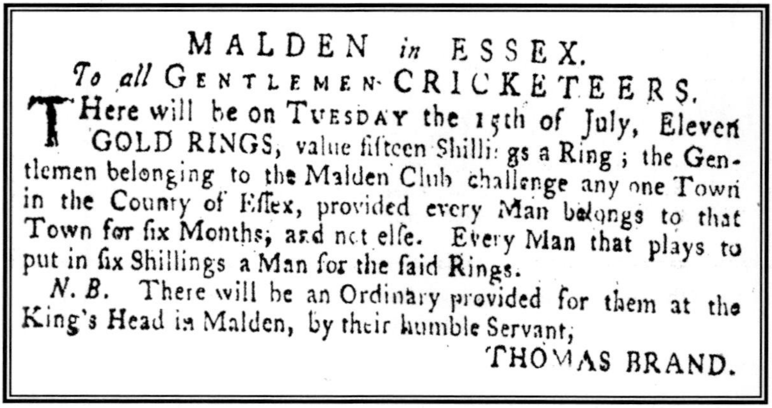
MALDEN *in* ESSEX.
To all GENTLEMEN-CRICKETEERS.
THere will be on TUESDAY the 15th of July, Eleven GOLD RINGS, value fifteen Shillings a Ring; the Gentlemen belonging to the Malden Club challenge any one Town in the County of Effex, provided every Man belongs to that Town for fix Months, and not elfe. Every Man that plays to put in fix Shillings a Man for the faid Rings.
N. B. There will be an Ordinary provided for them at the King's Head in Malden, by their humble Servant,
THOMAS BRAND.

2. Gentlemen Cricketeers. The story begins: Thomas Brand's notice in the *Ipswich Journal* of 5 July 1755.

for the game of 11 gold rings valued at 15 shillings each. Comparisons of money values are difficult but, as a guide, the prize could have been worth around £1500 today.

Unfortunately for Brand his new venture seemed to backfire. Although he must have had some encouragement from his customers connected with the cricket club, the public challenge offended some important people, including Pattison, the owner of the King's Head. Cricket was the preserve of the young gentlemen of Maldon, sons of wealthy merchants, who had both the time and the money to ape the fashions sweeping the upper classes. And those gentlemen drank at the Ship tavern on Fullbridge Street.

The Ship, run by John Edwick, was a short walk across the river Chelmer from Potman Marsh where cricket was played. The tavern was an oasis for gentlemen among the cluster of seven coarser alehouses catering for the tastes of sailors and dockworkers from the Fullbridge wharves, where Edwick had shipping interests. Unfortunately for Brand, Edwick was also a business partner of Pattison, who shared the freehold of the Ship.

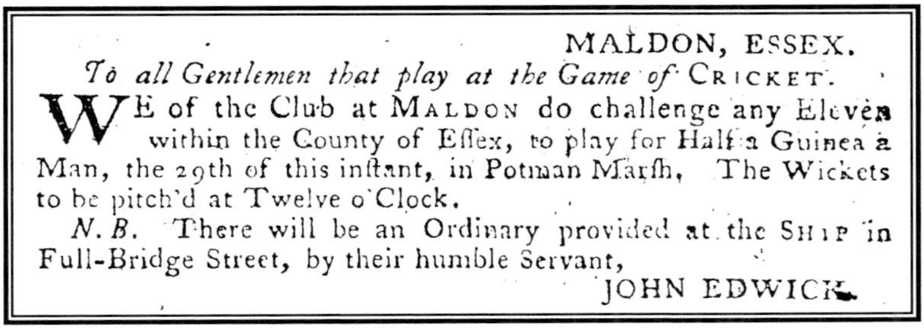

MALDON, ESSEX.

To all Gentlemen that play at the Game of CRICKET.

WE of the Club at MALDON do challenge any Eleven within the County of Eſſex, to play for Half a Guinea a Man, the 29th of this inſtant, in Potman Marſh, The Wickets to be pitch'd at Twelve o'Clock.

N. B. There will be an Ordinary provided at the SHIP in Full-Bridge Street, by their humble Servant,

JOHN EDWICK.

3. We of the club at Maldon. John Edwick's response to Brand's impertinence appeared in the *Ipswich Journal* on 23 August 1755.

Edwick and Pattison, evidently taking umbrage at Brand's presumption, used the *Ipswich Journal* to publish notices of their own. In August 1755, as if to assert the proper place of the Ship and Potman Marsh as the centre of Maldon cricket, Edwick's notice challenged any club within the county of Essex to play a game for 'half a guinea a man'. He specified 29 August for the contest at Potman Marsh, commencing at twelve noon.

Pattison's notice, published on 16 August, seemed to have more serious implications for Brand. It read as follows:

> To be let and entered upon at Michaelmas next The Kings Head Inn at Maldon situated in the best part of town with good cellars, good stabling and other conveniences. For further particulars enquire of Mr Joseph Pattison, *Merchant in Maldon.*

Could Pattison have been so seriously offended as to deprive Brand of his livelihood? Or was Brand restless and ready to move on? Certainly, few other openings for publicans could have been as lucrative as Maldon's King's Head and, if Brand was leaving on his own terms, why do so just a month after venturing into cricket promotion?

As for Edwick, there is no evidence of a response to his challenge but that was probably not his purpose. The proper social order had been restored and the gentlemen cricketers of

Maldon continued to bring their bats and balls to play on the marsh before limping across the Fullbridge at sunset for reviving drinks, tobacco and cards at the Ship tavern.

Chapter 2

The early matches 1771–75

Despite the challenges on behalf of the Maldon club in 1755, there are no reports of matches until the 1770s, when the *Chelmsford Chronicle* (established in 1764) began to publish accounts of games between clubs. During the intervening years the gentlemen cricketers doubtless played 'pick up' games on the marsh among themselves, with money prizes and side bets keeping the play keen.

The first reported match involving Maldon was played on 24 June 1771, against Stock, one of the more fashionable clubs of the day. In 1770, Eleven Gentlemen of Kent played on Stock Common and, on 13 June 1774, with the assistance of Mr Thomas Clark and Mr Bull, Stock beat the rest of Essex by 19 runs. Two days later they beat Gravesend 'with one picked man of Kent' by 77 runs.

The choice of opponents would have been important to Maldon's members as a means of confirming their high social standing in the county. Only Maldon, with Harwich and Colchester, were entitled to send members to parliament and, as a thriving seaport and market town, Maldon enjoyed high status in the region. Stock enjoyed high cricket status with a stake of 50 guineas (perhaps £10,000 today) a game regularly advanced by the club's wealthy patrons. Stock Common was also a venue for important matches such as that in 1785 between Hornchurch and the County of Essex.

Maldon's shipping area extended well into Hertfordshire and, in 1774, the cricket club played a game against Harlow that was lost 'with great odds'. The landlocked county town of Chelmsford was heavily dependent on Maldon's merchants but their cricket team also proved the stronger in 1775 when Maldon's innings of 45 for eight wickets in reply to 116, was saved by rain.

In 1774 there was a double wicket game against Two of Stock played on Danbury Common 'for a considerable sum of money'. The combative character and gambling potential of single and double wicket contests made them very popular, with mixed crowds of all classes flocking to enjoy the spectacle. The landlord of The Griffin met the clamour for ale and provided venison for the 'ordinary' (set lunch), as well as dinner for the members, players and guests.

This game provides the first record of players' names. Mr Lee and Mr Warner carried the Maldon colours against Mr Spight and Mr Berington for Stock. Wickets were pitched at 11 o'clock but the Maldon pair scored only 21 notches in their two innings, all scored by Mr Lee. The gentlemen of Stock proved far superior making 35 notches in a single innings. Dinner was taken at two o'clock.

By a strange coincidence, the names of Lee and Warner reappear 40 years later, as opening batsmen for East Essex against West Essex in 1817. The Shenfield turnpike road, running north to south, made the division of the county for the purpose and the game was played at Hornchurch Lane, Romford. East Essex 'gave up the game' when they needed 193 runs to win in the second innings, having been dismissed for 36 notches in the first. If these men were the sons or grandsons of the original double wicket contestants, they did not carry on the tradition of appearing for Maldon.

Although organized matches among clubs were becoming more common, the usual activity of the cricket club was the pick up match, where members simply met and played among themselves. Even the great Hambledon club only played about half a dozen organized matches a season and Maldon's few games against other clubs probably resulted from members looking to cement business or social relations with contacts in other towns.

The leading citizens of the town would run the clubs of the time. At Maldon it may have been the sons and grandsons of the wealthy merchants who carried the town's name onto the field of play, but it was the interests of their fathers and grandfathers that they represented. When prize money was at stake the senior members pledged it, when guest players were required to strengthen the team they met their expenses, when publicans promoted matches they underwrote them. In this way the cricket team was controlled to meet the social and commercial aspirations of the town, which had become a fashionable favourite even among well-to-do London families.

So it would continue despite shocks to the economic system that were looming on the horizon and would irreparably damage Maldon's standing in the southeast of England. But, for the time being, the gentlemen cricketers of Maldon played on regardless.

Chapter 3

The game on Potman Marsh

In the 1770s tricorn hats were fashionable on the cricket field although postilion caps of the style worn by coachmen were equally acceptable. There was no special cricket clothing and normal day wear was simply carried on to the field of play, providing colour and frills to enhance the spectacle of the early game. Shirts could be a variety of pastel colours and embroidered waistcoats were of intricate design. Knee length breeches were fastened over white silk stocking and buckled shoes. When Hambledon's John Wells tore off a fingernail on his shoe buckle in the 1780s, more practical ideas for footwear began to emerge.

Bats were much straighter than the 'hockey stick' design of the 1720s but there were no laws to regulate the size and shape. Maldon's players may have fashioned them from local timber or, more likely, paid a few pence to a carpenter to copy the latest model seen in use at fashionable London grounds. Whoever made it, the bat would have been shaped out of a single piece of timber, completed only with twine binding around the handle.

The straighter blade signals changes in methods of play. Early in the century the ball was trundled over rough ground, with the striker attempting to hit it away in the manner of a golf shot with a curved, bottom heavy bat. The straighter bat and rudimentary forward play evolved when bowlers began to lob the ball in the air to a length, and lunges across its line became more hazardous.

If bats could be of any shape and size under the laws, that was not the case with cricket balls: the first code of laws published in 1744 stipulated that 'The ball must weigh between five and six ounces' (compared with five and a half ounces

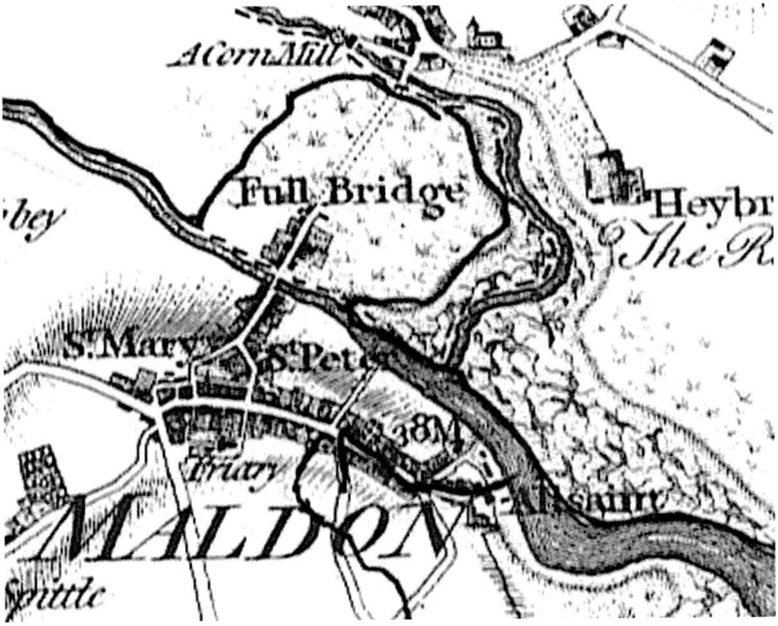

4. Potman Marsh at Fullbridge. The Chapman and Andre map of 1777 shows development at the busy Fullbridge wharf, but Potman Marsh is deserted saltings.

today). Moreover, their manufacture employed the same basic method as today: a cork centre bound with twine enclosed in a sewn leather casing.

Duke's balls were made in Kent and available for sale in the 1760s. They were finished with a triple hand sewn seam and advertised in newspapers and magazines at six shillings each (around £60 today). Perhaps the gentlemen cricketers of Maldon brought back these early Duke's balls from the London stores, although they may have produced them locally. The nearby village of Langford was a traditional centre for leather production and there were artisan cobblers in the town to copy the work of the Kent craftsmen.

How long these hand stitched balls lasted on the salting of

5. The Ship Tavern from Fullbridge wharf. The Ship is on the right at the bottom of Market Hill below the distinctive Maldon landmarks, St Peter's tower, the D'Arcy tower and All Saints' steeple.

Potman Marsh is anybody's guess. The surface of slow growing grass and weed had no prior preparation for play, with a suitable strip selected before commencement of each game. In an organized contest the captain winning the toss selected the strip to be used, whereupon wickets were pitched 22 yards apart and popping creases cut into the ground. The wicket under the 1744 laws comprised two stumps, 22 inches high, topped with a bail six inches long.

Around 1775 the third stump was added after Lumpy Stevens, playing for All England against Five of Hambledon, sent the ball three times through old John Small's stumps without removing the bail. It is not known how long the idea of using a third stump took to reach Maldon, but the great match involving Stevens and Small was played at the famous Artillery Ground in London, where Maldon's men of property frequented the clubs, coffee houses and assembly rooms.

The usual pick up games proceeded by dividing the playing members present into two teams, with late arrivals joining in by agreement. The toss and laying out of the pitch would proceed, as a stake for the game was agreed and side bets made. Two umpires were required under the laws to adjudicate dismissals as well as, 'all fair and unfair play, all frivolous delays, all hurts whether real or pretended', tasks made more difficult by the law that allowed either batter to hinder a catcher while the ball was in the air. Nevertheless, honesty and sportsmanship were paramount among the cricketers on pain of social isolation for lack of propriety.

There were no boundaries to the field of play with all hits being run and recorded as notches on a stick. Positioning of fielders had begun to conform to a pattern, with the wicket-keeper, short slip and point of the bat fielders forming an attacking arc behind the striker. Wicketkeepers wore no protective padding, which made the position of longstop a key defensive position. Long slip would patrol alongside him to field the snicks that passed the short fielders.

In front of the bat, fielders would occupy positions either in the short field or in the long field, depending upon the bowler's skill and the batter's hitting ability. The man at 'long field to cover middle wicket and point' required exceptional athletic ability, while long fields at 'straight on', 'straight off' and 'to the hip' were expected to run and catch. 'Middle wicket' at this time was in the short field to the off side of the striker, rather than the leg side in later years.

Methods of dismissal under the code of 1744 included those familiar today, such as bowled, caught, stumped, run out, hit wicket, hit the ball twice and handled the ball. Leg before wicket was not a specified mode of dismissal but umpires could deem that a batter was 'standing unfair to strike'. Umpires were also responsible for adjudicating good and bad runs and calling no balls if the bowler's back foot crossed the bowling crease before delivery.

Bowlers were required to deliver four-ball overs and could

change ends only once in an innings. Their greatest weapon, however, was to help select the playing strip after the toss, looking for ridges and hollows that would assist their bowling style. It was years later that Fuller Pilch, from Bury St Edmunds and the greatest English batsman of his generation, tried to counter this advantage to bowlers by carrying his own scythe to cut the grass!

By the 1780s many familiar features of the modern game were established. The general conduct of the game, methods of dismissal, fair and unfair play were all covered by the early laws and they had begun to adapt to meet new circumstances. Cricket at Hambledon set the standards for the age, but with Maldon's merchant population highly mobile in the southeast of England and newspapers circulating freely, best practice spread quickly to the home county.

Chapter 4

Cricket in town and village 1780–1800

By the 1780s cricket was played in town and village throughout the region. In Pycroft's classic book *The Cricket Field*, he recounts a conversation with old players from Essex and Kent, who were boys in 1785. Cricket, they said, was played in every school and village green in Essex and Kent: 'There was a cricket bat behind the door, or else up in the bacon rack, in every cottage.'

Reports in the *Chelmsford Chronicle* suggest that by this time the Maldon club was playing several matches, presumably for the customary prize money, each season. In 1784 they met Chelmsford three times between June and September, two of the games on Potman Marsh, and beat them twice.

The following year the gentlemen cricketers took horse and carriage 15 miles along the northern Blackwater shore to meet the club of East & West Mersea. That game, played on 21 July was unfinished but arrangements were made to complete the contest on 1 August. The result is not recorded but there was time for a second match to be played out on the same day.

The practice of deferring matches to ensure a result appears to have become quite common at this time. Completion of an unfinished game against Boreham in July 1786 was deferred after Maldon had scored 116 and 122 runs and Boreham had made 69 and 28 runs for six wickets in their second innings. The completion was scheduled for September, leaving two months of suspense before Maldon tried to take the remaining four wickets needed for victory. Also in 1786, Maldon lost to

Purleigh by 28 'notches' – a result that rankled the members and led to a series of money matches in future years.

It was also in 1786 that the first detailed scorecard of a Maldon match was published. Playing at Ingatestone on 28 August, Maldon lost the game, scoring 36 and 21 runs in response to the home team's 27 and 81 runs. The report of the return match, played at Potman Marsh on 12 September (see scorecard at end of chapter), provides an interesting contemporary account of a club cricket match:

> On Tuesday, September 12, the return match of cricket was played at Maldon, between Ingatestone, in conjunction with several adjacent parishes, and Mr Thomas Clarke, of Arnolds; against the Maldon cricket club; about half-past five, a very heavy storm of wind and rain prevented the game being decided that evening. Consequently it was renewed next morning, when it terminated in favour of the former. Maldon first innings was attended with several unfortunate accidents, which made it short; after Ingatestone's first innings, many bets were offered at very large odds, and as freely accepted, that Ingatestone would beat in one innings; but as it proved contrary to the *knowing* ones' expectation, considerable sums were lost, so that the odds taken were in general thought greatly to exceed the original bets.
>
> The behaviour of Mr Clarke deserves the highest applause as a gentleman, and lover of the noble game of cricket, in which he so eminently excels.

At the end of the 1786 season the gentlemen of the cricket club celebrated with a dinner. John Crosier, the Beeleigh miller, who rode the mile along the southern bank of the river Chelmer to enjoy the hospitality of the Ship tavern, recorded in his diary for that year, 'At the finishing of the season they din'd in the Assembly room, 58 in number, when mirth and festivity flourish'd, and Bacchus began his jollity for the Winter season.'

During 1787 and 1788 Maldon won three and lost two games against Purleigh, but it was matches against Coggeshall in 1788 that caught the headlines and remind us that bad behaviour on the field is not a modern phenomenon. Monday 28 July was a fine, sunny day and a large crowd had assembled on Potman Marsh to watch the Maldon club contest the honours with new visitors from Coggeshall. The betting before play was heavy but the anticipation of the spectators was soon tinged with disappointment as a poor game developed. Maldon scored 82 and 66 runs in their two innings but Coggeshall replied weakly with only 29 runs in their first innings. At 25 runs for five wickets in their second innings the report says they 'gave up the game'.

Conceding a game was almost unthinkable bearing in mind that bets could ride on individual scores, team totals, margins of win, and other more imaginative factors. There must have been some unusual circumstance behind the decision of the Coggeshall captain to refuse to play 'at the peril of giving (up) the game'. Certainly, there was no improvement in sporting relations between the two teams when they met at Coggeshall for the return match on 2 September when, after the first innings there was a difference of only five notches between the scores. Then one of the Maldon players committed the ultimate crime by refusing to accept the umpire's decision. The *Morning Herald* carried the following report of the incident:

> A dispute prevented the game being played out as the Maldon players refused to abide by the umpire's decision. After waiting the time limited by the articles, the game was declared to be lost on the part of Maldon.

The clubs did not meet again for nearly 100 years.

During the 1790s the Maldon club won two more games against Purleigh and beat Chelmsford comfortably by five wickets. In another eventful game, Chelmsford were strengthened by players from Writtle, Boreham, Ongar and Great

Baddow, but the match was undecided after a Chelmsford player was taken ill and bad light caused play to be abandoned. In a single wicket competition on Writtle Green in July 1795, Mr Prescott of Chelmsford scored 32 and 19 runs, thrashing Mr Mitchell of Maldon who offered a paltry single run in his two innings!

Rochford Hundred and Winstree Hundred were added to the Maldon club's regular opponents, together with Tolleshunt Major and the neighbouring Dengie Hundred. Against Dengie in 1790, the men of the Hundred started as 2 to 1 favourites to win the match, but Maldon confounded the bookmakers with a seven wickets victory (Dengie Hundred 71 and 50 runs; Maldon 57 and 65 runs with three wickets down). A match with Winstree Hundred on 29 July 1800 was described as 'an excellent and friendly game, terminated in favour of Maldon with nine wickets to go down'.

Playing against the Maldon club for Winstree Hundred was Joseph Page, a farmer from West House Farm at Fingringhoe, who recorded in his diary:

> Played cricket on Abberton Green with ten others against eleven of Maldon, but got beat. The first innings there was but three runs difference in favour of Maldon, but the second innings they got with great ease.

Page also records in his diary that he played at Maldon on 7 August in a match his team lost by 57 runs, but Waghorn in *The Dawn of Cricket* reckons that match was played on 15/16 September. Farmer Page's diary, however, shows he was sailing and shooting on those dates.

Although cricket had continued unabated since the outbreak of the French revolutionary wars in 1793, after 1800 reports disappeared almost completely from newspapers and magazines as renewed hostilities from France and the threat of internal civil unrest began to occupy the national consciousness.

Maldon versus Ingatestone, 12 September 1786

Ingatestone

First innings		*Second innings*	
Mr Goldstone b Limbner	3		
W. Hogg b Limbner	19		
Graves b Rumble	11		
J. Dawson c Polley	4		
T. Dawson b Rumble	2		
W. Dawson b Limbner	2		
Clarke b Rumble	13	not out	12
Burrell c Rush	15	not out	13
Coverdale c Limbner	18		
J. Hogg run out	21		
Clay not out	4	extras	5
	109*		**30**

Total for both innings **139**

Maldon

Mr Pond run out	7	b Graves	14
Mitchell c Burrell	0	c W. Hogg	10
Limbner b Graves	14	b Graves	0
Rumble b Burrell	1	c J. Dawson	16
White b Graves	0	put out by Clarke	18
Edwards b Graves	3	b Burrell	3
Winn not out	7	b Graves	1
Cotty beat down wicket	14	b Coverdale	2
Rush b Graves	0	not out	2
Polley b Burrell	0	c Clay	26
Drake c J. Dawson	0	c W. Dawson	0
	46		**92**

Total for both innings **138**

* Scores actually total 112, but arithmetical errors were common in old newspapers. Majority for Ingatestone, ten wickets.

Chapter 5

War and depression 1800–1837

After 1800 there are no further reports of cricket matches played by the Maldon club until 1814, when they met Winstree Hundred again on Potman Marsh. Nationally, there was a similar decline in the popularity of cricket according to the record of matches contained in Haygarth's *Scores and Biographies*. Many ideas have been advanced for the decline, mostly linked to the harsh consequences of the industrial revolution, the threat of civil unrest and the shadow of invasion by France.

If Maldon was still untouched by the factory systems of the industrial Midlands, it was certainly not unaffected by the rise of Napoleon. Essex ports were prime targets for invasion and strategically important for the shipment of troops and supplies to the continent. Nearby Danbury Park and Tiptree Common served as important army barracks and troops were garrisoned in Maldon itself. The war, however, was good for trade, particularly for Maldon's farmers who reaped unprecedented profits from artificially high corn prices. Conversely, the price of corn forced the labouring classes towards starvation.

In their desperation starving families were forced into criminal protest, and began setting fire to ricks and barns at farms in Maldon, Dengie, Thurstable and beyond. The authorities feared this sort of civil unrest was symptomatic of the revolution in France and miscreants were transported or, as in the case of 16-year-old James Cook, executed. The same fear of insurrection made the authorities suspicious of any large public gathering, including the crowds that had become customary at cricket matches at the turn of the century.

The grim mood of the nation was reflected through the columns of the *Chelmsford Chronicle*. The accounts of cricket matches, horse races, cockfights, theatre and balls gave way to dour reports of military campaigns abroad and political affairs at home. That is not to say, of course, that people stopped enjoying themselves, merely that life's frivolities became much less public. Cricket undoubtedly continued, if not in an organized way by the Maldon club then certainly by the officers commanding local garrisons and billeted in the town.

On occasions cricket became a serious matter as the game at Maldon reported in the *Bury and Norwich Post* of 21 June 1809 testifies.

> Ensign P. Mohan and Assistant Surgeon Lewis O'Hara, both of the Eleventh Regiment of Foot, fell into argument over a small point during a game. The dispute escalated to the point that honour could only be satisfied by the ancient tradition of pistols at dawn. Against the rising sun at a secret venue outside the town, the two soldiers paced their distances, turned and fired.

O'Hara's shot missed its target but the army was a doctor short when Ensign Mohan's bullet hit him between the eyes.

After the allied victory at Waterloo in 1815 reports of cricket matches began to increase. The *Chelmsford Chronicle*, in the edition of 15 August 1817, rejoiced 'to see a spirit for this noble game reviving in this County'.

On Monday 15 August 1817 Maldon returned to Stock Common to play the local club, probably for 100 guineas. Play commenced at ten o'clock and dinner was taken at the Bear inn. In 1819, the Maldon club played twice against Pattiswick for 100 guineas and twice against Chelmsford for the same stake. Play commenced at nine o'clock in these matches but results are unknown, except for the second match at Chelmsford on

31 August. The home club scored 45 and 62 runs in their innings and, when Maldon had made eight runs with no wickets down in their second innings, 'the majority was obtained and the voices of the scorers proclaimed the game won'.

Although cricket had reappeared, life in Maldon had by no means returned to prewar normality. Falling prices hit trade and farmers in particular suffered from reduced prices for corn. Nor did cheaper grain rescue the starving labourers because landowners, in an effort to restore income, increased rents to tenants who, in turn, reduced wages and laid off workers. There followed years of depression in agriculture during which incidents of arson increased and penniless workers were forced into the new workhouses.

Not only had the agricultural element of Maldon's economy collapsed but the decline of the seaport had also begun. In 1797, amid concerted protest by Maldon's great and good, the Chelmer Navigation canal opened between Heybridge and Springfield to provide a direct waterway to Chelmsford. The effect was to bypass the established wharves at Maldon and enhance the County town as a distribution centre for Essex and Hertfordshire.

Despite the changes, Maldon remained a fashionable town, with good livings to be made by the versatile merchants, skilled craftsmen and professional men, who now played cricket. During the 1820s the names of Tomlinson and Devenish first appear on Maldon team sheets. Dick Devenish played an influential part in the powerful side that developed in the last years on Potman Marsh, and the family name lived on in local cricket until the 1960s. Thomas Tomlinson, a son of the original player, took Maldon to unprecedented heights of esteem during the 1870s.

Two matches were played against Chelmsford in 1820 but the results were not reported. The game at Chelmsford was played on Oxney Green, where Mr Lewis of the Spotted Dog provided refreshments. The match at Langley Park against Great Waltham in 1826 was preceded by an eight o'clock breakfast at the Six Bells that sustained the Maldon men sufficiently to achieve a win by nine wickets.

Meanwhile, in 1824, Maldon lost to Fryerning at Ingatestone, scoring 39 and 71 runs against the home team's 49 and 67 runs. The team that played in this match was Barker, the brothers Bygrave, M. Cottee, R. Cottee, Devenish, Drake, Drowley, Joslin, Tomlinson and Wright. From the first known team that played in 1786, only the name of Cottee (then spelt Cotty) survived.

The first of a long series of matches with Witham began in 1828, when Maldon won twice. During the 1830s Kelvedon and Writtle (then 'descending in status') were added to the list of opponents and games continued against old rivals, Stock. As well as seeing a return to widespread popularity, the 1830s also brought some important changes into cricket, notably the legalisation of round arm bowling in 1835. In response to this change, improvised padding began to be used to protect batsmen from the faster deliveries on rough ground. To further increase the advantage of bowlers, wickets increased in size to 27 by 8 inches and the bat was restricted to modern proportions of 38 by 4¼ inches. The tinkering with the lbw. law was also begun by the Marylebone Cricket Club (MCC), which had grown into the legislative body for the game.

The heavy betting that had characterised the early game had led to some shameful corruptions and match fixing. Young country players engaged for Lord's matches were regularly bribed by bookmakers in their London lodgings and, in one instance, a player was diverted from play by a false report that his wife had died. Umpires were allowed to bet on the outcome of matches and generally the propriety of cricket had sunk to an all time low.

When bookmakers were banned from Lords in the 1820s a clear signal was given of the MCC's intention to clean up the game. Although no scandals arising from Maldon's money matches were ever reported, the change of mood among the new cricket establishment spelled an end to such games and the

6. Potman Marsh in the twentieth century. After the railways came and Sadd's timber wharves grew to support international trade, there was little room left for a game of cricket.

frenzy of betting that had accompanied them. By 1837 and the accession of Queen Victoria the stage was set for the version of the game in which honour and fair play were paramount.

Part 2

Victorian Summers

Chapter 6

The Victorian cricket club 1980

For the first decade of Queen Victoria's reign, Maldon continued to play on Potman Marsh, although the land had been sold at auction in 1840. The club had shifted its headquarters from the Ship tavern on the hill to the Queen Victoria in Mill Lane, where William and Mary Keys and their teenage servants, Charlotte and Sarah, provided the hospitality. During a game against Kelvedon in 1841, which Maldon won on first innings, lunch was served on the ground at three o'clock and, at seven o'clock, the company adjourned to the Victoria and, 'kept the harmony and conviviality up to rather a late hour'.

Such was the impact of the young Queen that public houses throughout the land – and several in Maldon – renamed themselves in her honour. The fashion spread to the cricket club in 1845 when it styled itself 'Maldon Victoria' before reverting to Maldon Town Cricket Club on the move to the Fairfield in 1848. The club was finally forced from Potman Marsh by the industrialisation of the riverside after private owners acquired the area at the 1840 auction. John Sadd bought land for the extension of his shipping and timber business that would become one of Maldon's two major employers but, in the 1840s, Sadd's legal battle with Eastern Counties Railway over the Maldon terminus for the Braintree and Witham line soaked up most of the firm's capital.

By the time the railway finally opened in October 1848, the club had enjoyed a first season on the Fairfield that commenced with great optimism. The *Chelmsford Chronicle* had pronounced in May:

> There is every prospect of this manly game being carried on here with spirit this season. In consequence of the old ground (Potman Marsh) being required for the railway, the Victoria Club has been dissolved and a new one established under the name of Maldon Town Cricket Club – it already musters upwards of 50 members. The opening game was played on Monday last, in the fair field and should the present fine weather continue it is expected there will be a match played before the end of the month as the club is willing to enter into a game with any club within 16 or 17 miles of the town.

In the event, only matches home and away against Witham and Danbury were reported in 1848, none of which Maldon won.

The move to the Fairfield, the ground off Fambridge Road that is still used today by the Upper Plume School, presented a golden opportunity for the club to modernise. Round-arm bowling had been legalised in 1835 and probably proved dangerous on the natural surface of Potman Marsh. The incoming high arm style might have led to serious injuries. Nor would the saltings have responded significantly to the new methods of pitch preparation that emerged following the invention of the lawnmower. Edward Budding's design of 1830 incorporated all the principles on which modern mowers are built. In particular, the rotating cylinder of blades replaced the hand held scythe and produced a smoother finish than ever before. A rear roller that left an even finer surface replaced the trampling feet of scythe wielding mowers.

By 1833 Ransomes of Ipswich were manufacturing Budding's 'patent grass-cutting machine' and advertisements appeared in magazines and local newspapers. In the 1860s Maldon's second (after Sadds) major industrial employer, E. H. Bentall, was making lawnmowers and cast iron rollers were also widely available. When Frank Silcock became Maldon's professional in 1861, his duties included that of groundsman, operating the mechanical equipment the club had doubtless purchased for the care of the Fairfield's turf.

The short life of the Victoria Club was not ended out of disloyalty to the monarch, but in order to cut the ties with the Victoria inn when the move from Potman Marsh took the club to the White Horse at the top of the High Street. This 'ancient rendezvous for cricketers' run by William Samms became the clubhouse, a status protected by the club rules, where general meetings were held on the first Monday of each month during the season. General meetings considered applications for membership and match fixtures. Membership was closely controlled with nominations received at one meeting being decided at the next. A two-thirds majority vote was necessary to admit a new member and, as a further safeguard, his nominee who remained responsible for his conduct paid his ten shillings subscription.

Of Maldon's 50 or so members, the majority would be drawn from leading civic and business figures who would lend social and financial standing to the club. Most would never play, even in the pick-up matches for which the ground was available every day, but they would draw kudos from important matches attended by leading figures in the county. The cricket club was stitched into the social fabric of the town, with the Reverend Horwood, Member of Parliament, George Sandford, and County Magistrate J. Oxley-Parker making up the presidency of the club in 1867. The initiative for the All England Eleven match in 1873 came from town notables William Humpherys and Henry Sprague, whose influence on cricket never extended to playing it. Cricketers like Thomas Tomlinson and Alfred Self became borough councillors, while notorious sportsman and adventurer, Sir Claude Champion de Crespigny, who lived nearby was drawn into club affairs.

For those members who wanted to play cricket, selection was by committee appointed by the first general meeting each season. The president, vice-presidents, honorary treasurer and honorary secretary were joined sometimes by up to 12 further members to pick the teams for matches. There were probably no more than about six matches in an average season and these were always played on weekdays. The Fairfield was available for practice games on any day of the week and non-members were allowed to participate. This allowed local players who had caught the eye to be invited to trial games to assess their suitability for membership of the town club.

The general meeting in May considered match fixtures. The honorary secretary would read out letters from clubs wanting to make a match and the meeting would decide which clubs were of appropriate standing. Matches were not arranged far in advance since the rules of the club required that 'all expenses of previous match be paid' before further games were organized. In 1852, when no suitable applications for matches were received, Maldon was forced to advertise its willingness to meet clubs within 16 miles of the town. It seems as if the club was always careful to set its catchment area to include the prestigious club at Colchester.

In 1866 the general meeting set the first match for Thursday 17 May, although no opposition was specified and no reports later appeared. Matches against Colchester and Witham were agreed on a 'home and home' basis and a much bigger list of fixtures than usual was arranged. Clarence Amateurs were beaten at the 'Eton & Middlesex Ground at Primrose Hill' and there were four games at Orsett, against Romford, Southend, Hoo (Kent) and Mr Jolly's Eleven. Matches were also arranged on their own grounds against Hoo, Romford and Mr Jolly at Aveley.

These opponents did not feature again as Maldon preferred the fashionable circuit closer to home, although it did begin to venture more frequently into London as its reputation grew. Social position in the nineteenth century remained crucially important and the gentlemen of Maldon strove to ensure that their club was among the elite. There were no structures for selecting county or national teams and Essex would not enter the county championship until 1895. By maintaining its standing Maldon could attract talented cricketers with the promise of competition against leading players in the county under the watchful eye of influential patrons of the Victorian game.

Chapter 7

Country house cricket

The cricket house party was a Victorian institution. Wealthy families would lay out cricket grounds at their country properties, if only to occupy their sons when they came home from school for the summer holidays. More serious exponents of the game would invite friends of their older sons to stay and make up cricket teams, while young lady acquaintances of their daughters would stay in the hope of striking suitable matches with the men. For competitive matches, formidable arrays of talent could be assembled with leading professionals frequently engaged to play.

Maldon was rich in country house venues. Woodham Mortimer Place, Down Hall, Bradwell and Baddow Hall, Great Baddow, were within a short carriage ride, as were the more elite Felix Hall, home of Lord Western at Kelvedon, and Charles Du Cane's extensive property at Braxted Park. In 1870 Maldon reached the top of the tree with a match at Lord Petre's exclusive Thorndon Hall, where the colourful and talented wandering sides of the period were frequent guests.

Woodham Mortimer Place was the home of Mr Oxley-Parker, a banker, magistrate and vice-president of Maldon Cricket Club. Maldon's first recorded match there was played in 1859, when Henry Gower, a talented young player who would be a mainstay of the club for many years, made his debut. Thereafter the match became an annual event until 1870 with many talented players and men of means enjoying the play and the generous hospitality. When taking a team to play against other country landowners, Oxley-Parker would usually include some of the better-heeled Maldon players.

Many notable cricketers played at Braxted Park, the home

of Charles Du Cane, who represented Maldon in Parliament for eight months until his election was quashed for corrupt practices in March, 1853. Du Cane was later elected as Member for Colchester and eventually became Governor of Tasmania, receiving a knighthood for his services. Educated at Charterhouse and Exeter College, Oxford, he was a good enough batsman to represent the MCC and the early Essex teams.

His brother Alfred was a slow round-arm bowler, who played for Cambridge in the University matches of 1854 and 1855. The brothers played together in Braxted Park matches, as well as for local clubs, Witham and, during a period of fashionable ascendancy, Layer-de-la-Haye. They played a game for Maldon, against Upton Amicables in 1855, but did nothing of particular distinction.

Maldon played at Braxted Park in 1864 when Frank Silcock was its professional. Silcock did not waste the opportunity to demonstrate his prowess in front of influential spectators, scoring 50 and bowling magnificently. Such performances in front of the right people were essential for the ambitious cricketer and helped Silcock to progress from the local circuit to the Essex team. Later he would play for the United South of England Eleven and for the Players against the Gentlemen at Lords.

Less grand than the Du Canes, the Page family were farmers at Down Hall, Bradwell. Two brothers, Robert and Joseph, played for Maldon between 1850 and 1870, also appearing alongside various other Maldon regulars for Tillingham, Bradwell and Dengie Hundred, as well in Mr Page's country-house Eleven at Down Hall. Page was well connected in Essex cricket circles and brought many fine and influential players and guests to Bradwell to meet Maldon, who would be styled for the engagement as 'Mr Tomlinson's Eleven'.

Tomlinson, the personality behind Maldon's most successful years of cricket, no doubt forged many influential friendships while playing at Down Hall where, said the *Chelmsford Chronicle* there was a 'large circle of friends and visitors who

7. Country house cricket. Down Hall, Bradwell where the greats of Essex cricket assembled to meet Mr Tomlinson's Maldon Eleven.

are invariably attracted to this delightful spot'. Mr Page's Eleven versus Mr Tomlinson's Eleven became an annual August event. Page's Eleven were also invited to play at Woodham Mortimer Place and at Mr Turner's Baddow Hall. Invariably, Page would invite the respectable nucleus of the Maldon club to play in his team.

Another talented young Maldon cricketer destined to play for Essex was Charles Escott, whose father had moved from London to Tillingham's parish church of St Nicholas in 1859. After some distinguished performances for both club and country-house elevens, Escott began to lead his own invitation eleven and was engaged in a peculiar match in 1869.

Playing at Mr Page's Down Hall ground, Escott's Eleven batted first against Peldon. In an age when team totals were usually less than 100, either the Down Hall pitch was exceptionally good or the Peldon bowling was exceptionally bad for, as the *Chelmsford Chronicle* reported:

> Mr Escott's eleven commenced their innings at 11.30 and when stumps were drawn at seven o'clock had nine wickets down for 553 runs

Because pitches were generally poor and scores low, the laws of cricket did not include provision for declarations. Until changed in 1889, the laws obliged a team to keep batting until it was bowled out.

No other matches at the country house grounds were as bizarre as Escott's. Usually they were sparkling social occasions accompanied by high quality cricket, such as that at Woodham Mortimer Place in 1867, when Escott played for Page's Eleven alongside Tomlinson, the Page brothers and Dyke from Maldon. Oxley-Parker had lined up some of the cream of Essex cricket against them, including Fane, Gepp, Owen and, most famously, James and Francis Round.

James Round, a key figure in the history of Essex cricket, was a wicket-keeper batsman of the highest class who played for the Gentlemen against the Players at both Lords and the Oval in 1867. He was behind the formation of the Essex county club at Brentwood in 1876 and captained the team until 1882. Francis, his younger brother, also appeared in the early Essex team at Brentwood.

Not surprisingly, Page's Eleven lost the game, replying with just 67 to a total of 152, mostly scored by Pearson, Fane and Francis Round.

Unperturbed, Page took advantage of Oxley-Parker's generous hospitality after the match to persuade Francis Round to bring a team to play at Down Hall later in the season. The match took place in September and provided the most colourful occasion that Page's Bradwell home had ever seen.

The *Chelmsford Chronicle* reported that Down Hall was graced by:

> Numbers of ladies, whose summer dresses contrasted pleasingly with the fantastic uniforms of the Knickerbockers, the Calves, the Colchester and other clubs, whose representatives were engaged in the match.

One notable cricketer so engaged was Charles Green, a magnificent all-round sportsman who, like Charles Round, had represented the Gentlemen against the Players. He was engaged by Middlesex, but took over as captain of Essex when Round gave it up in 1882. He became, perhaps, the most significant figure in the history of Essex cricket when he masterminded the move from Brentwood to Leyton and secured entry for Essex into the County Championship in 1895.

At Down Hall in 1867, Green was bowled by Maldon's Henry Gower for six, after another future Essex player, Charles Ridley, had been run out for a 'duck'. Two military men, Captains Curtis and Player, repaired some of the damage but Round's team was bowled out by Escott and Gower for 83. Maldon's Copsey and Colchester's Cant top scored in the reply of 76 before the opposition, batting a second time, scored 101. Gepp made 58 and Escott, Gower and Cant shared the wickets. Twilight intervened to leave the match unfinished, and the company retired to enjoy 'the warm hospitality of the popular captain of the Down Hall team'.

In 1870 Maldon were invited to the exclusive ground at Thorndon Hall. The host, Lord Petre, included the MCC, I Zingari, Free Foresters and Incogniti among his guests that summer. Between them, these clubs could field the very best amateur cricketers of the day. Maldon fielded an unexceptional team consisting of Tomlinson, John and Joseph Beale, Dyke, Escott, Henry and James Gower, Page, Self, Sewell and Timperley.

Against them Thorndon Hall had engaged the former Maldon professional, Frank Silcock, his cousin Joe, a professional from Bishops Stortford, and John Bristow, a left arm bowler playing for Surrey. Amateurs included Baker, Boardman and Nicholas, all of whom represented Essex in the first season of the new county club at Brentwood in 1876. Their combined efforts against Tomlinson's lobs and the bowling of Timperley brought a total of only 67 runs, whereupon Maldon, in a fine team effort, made 136. In their second innings Lord Petre's team made 134 but the match was awarded to Maldon on first innings.

This victory achieved by genuinely local Maldon men over a high calibre representative team was probably one of the great wins in the town's cricket history. It is unfortunate that it does not appear to have earned Maldon any further invitations from Lord Petre.

The traditional country cricket house party remained popular well into the twentieth century but, by then, its significance was mostly social as structures for selecting county and national teams had been put in place. When Maldon's Silcock and Escott were making their way in the game of the 1860s, country house matches were an essential part of the loosely structured world of cricket on which they had to make their mark.

Chapter 8
Clubs, pubs and grounds

During the 250 years of cricket at Maldon, the town club has appeared in several different guises and many smaller clubs have come and gone in and around the town. In Victorian times, changes of title and the creation of splinter clubs often mirrored public fashions and concerns of the day.

As far back as 1779, the bachelors of Maldon challenged, 'the bachelors of any town in Essex, the players to have resided there twelve months' to a match. It is not clear how the bachelors related to the Maldon club, but the challenge was issued from the White Lion on the opposite side of Market Hill to the Ship, where John Crosier noted in his diary that the members of the cricket club, 'smok'd their pipes and play'd at cards', while 'a regular set played the game in the marsh'.

The bachelors were in action again in 1846, but this time clearly as part of the Maldon club in a match between the married and single members. Reports of such matches were common at all levels of the game and the one of the matches on Potman Marsh gives the names of the Maldon players:

> For the Married men – Beckwith, Beale, Cottee, Elston, Battle, Keys (sen.), Keys (jun.), R. Devenish, Clarke, Otway and Miles.
>
> For the Single men – Banks, Bulley, Codd, W. Devenish, Driffield, Hurrell, Payne, Rumsey, Tavener, Tomlinson and Waring.

During the last days on Potman Marsh the club, in common with many others, styled themselves 'Victoria' in homage to the young Queen. They also took refreshment at the Queen Victoria inn in Mill Lane that was probably renamed from the Hoy alehouse, the favourite haunt of sailors the century before. In 1861 against Tillingham, the club adopted the title 'Maldon Amity'. This was another common device used at the time to denote a friendly encounter that did not employ the full powers of an established club against weaker or untried opponents.

In the 1870s, Maldon Amateurs came into existence and boasted a membership of 50 by 1889. Again, there was a general movement towards this style of club, possibly as a reaction against the over serious attitudes of established clubs or, perhaps simply because those clubs restricted membership by their election procedures. Maldon Amateurs played on a pitch at the rifle range ground against local clubs like Heybridge and Langford and against Maldon Second Eleven. The club's second eleven had first appeared in 1867, playing a game against Heybridge.

In 1871, Maldon Temperance cricket club appeared. The Temperance movement had crossed the Atlantic from America in the 1830s to campaign against the excessive drinking that was blighting many sections of British society. The formation of a Temperance cricket club at Maldon was presumably a comment on the drinking and carousing associated with the town club's matches. Several minor players from the town club switched their allegiance to the new club, which also provided another playing opportunity for people excluded from town club membership. As well as campaigning against excessive drinking, the Temperance Society was a champion of working class culture and the formation of the cricket club at Maldon came at a time when factory employment was rapidly expanding. Although the history is sketchy, it may well be that the Temperance club was a forerunner of Maldon Wesleyans, which itself became Maldon Strollers Cricket Club in 1932.

Works cricket was widely played with paternalistic employers providing facilities for the welfare of their employees.

Bentall's games were played on land that subsequently became the home of Heybridge Swifts football club and is now the Bentall Centre. Sadd's ground was on a northern part of Potman Marsh, behind the seawall protecting it from Heybridge Creek, an area also used for light industry today. Sadd's matches were less widely reported but, in 1889, they did play a match against Maldon Ironworks, another important local industry operated from the premises now occupied by the Sportsman social club.

In 1848 a match was played between teams from Bentall's entitled 'Capital versus Labour'. At this time social unease about working conditions in the industrial north was at its height and Karl Marx published the 'Communist Manifesto', predicting revolution by the working classes against the capital owners. It seems curiously inflammatory now to have so divided the workforce for a cricket match but Bentall obviously believed in clear demarcation between the classes. Presumably he also believed that the paternalistic values that drove his factory system would breed satisfied workers who would entertain no thoughts of revolution.

The terms never appeared again, however, with later games styled 'Office versus Works', with Maldon's Ashley and the Beales representing the white collars workers. There was also a full departmental programme of cricket matches with teams representing the Fitters, the Blacksmiths, the Foundrymen and the Turners all playing against each other.

As well as factory matches, cricket flourished at Heybridge and the surrounding villages, practically all of which could muster a team. Even the hamlet of Heybridge Basin, where the Chelmer canal terminated and the firm of Blackwater Timbers grew, arranged Saturday matches against local teams. The club at Heybridge that would later eclipse Maldon's standing for a time, was established by the 1850s when it played at 'Mr Sadler's ground' against most other local clubs.

Claude Champion de Crespigny, the 'Sporting Essex Baronet' laid out a cricket ground at his home off Broad Street

Green at Heybridge. De Crespigny, a sporting adventurer who later became a patron of the Maldon club, served with the King's Royal Rifles in India and became a passionate exponent of steeplechasing, boxing and shooting, on which he frittered away his considerable family inheritance. He nevertheless found funds to buy the house built by E. H. Bentall that he renamed 'Champion Lodge' where he hosted cricket matches (an elderly person's home today).

Towards the end of the Victorian era cricket was more popular than ever with numerous clubs providing matches for the large population of working people who inhabited the town.

Chapter 9

Maldon versus Colchester 1844–1868

As the fortunes of other clubs waxed and waned as the years passed, Colchester remained a strong and fashionable centre for cricket. Reference to cricket at Colchester first appeared in 1749 and in 1751 it challenged any eleven to meet at the Pig inn at Botolph's Gate to play for eleven black velvet caps. One hundred years later, Colchester was attracting many of the County's leading players, to the extent that, in 1865, a county club of Essex was formed at Colchester's new ground off Wimpole Lane. By this time Maldon had acquired the status to claim the Colchester club as regular opponents.

The first recorded match was played in 1844, when William Beckwith bowled his round arm 'steam shot' deliveries with Richard Devenish employing a hop, skip and jump action for his left arm seamers. Colchester was demolished and Maldon compiled one of the highest scores of their history to date (see scorecard on next page).

The victory did nothing to endear Maldon to the Colchester club and it was 1855 before they returned to Maldon to play at the Fairfield. Charles Du Cane and the Hon. F. Grimston were among a powerful Colchester team of 'good men and true', but Maldon were below strength 'owing to the indisposition of one or two of their best men'. The Kent professional, William Goodhew, had, however been employed for the match and the Reverend Frederick Thackeray, a former Cambridge blue and Hertfordshire amateur, made a rare appearance for Maldon. Thanks to Goodhew and the 'slashing hitting of Mr George Hurrell' Maldon made 71 runs in their first inning before bowling Colchester out for 36 runs. Goodhew and Cooper each took five wickets and, as there was no time to play out the second innings, Maldon were awarded the match.

Maldon versus Colchester, played on Potman Marsh, 30 July 1844

Colchester			*Maldon*		
Randolph	b. Beckwith	2	W. Devenish	b. Pargeter	72
Pargeter	b. Beckwith	0	Beckwith	b. Randolph	8
Nice	run out	1	Rush	b. T. Nunn	28
Rooke	b. Beckwith	3	Payne	st. Randolph	1
Raven	b. Beckwith	11	Fairhead	b. Pargeter	20
Young	c. Payne	0	Waring	b. Randolph	6
T. Nunn	b. Devenish	3	Rumsey	b. Pargeter	0
P. Nunn	b. Beckwith	0	R. Devenish	not out	16
Rowe	b. Beckwith	2	Blanks	Not out	26
Cant	b. Beckwith	3			
Barnes	not out	0			
Extras	Byes 18, wides 6	24	Extras	Byes 15, wides 7	22
	Total	**48**		**Total for 7 wickets**	**199**

The spirit of this game had been good and such was the mutual respect between the clubs that a return match was agreed later in the season. It was played on the Ordnance Field at Colchester, with lunch provided in the old powder magazine that had been specially adapted for the purpose. Goodhew was again engaged for the match and he, with assistance from Tomlinson and Lawrence, bowled out Colchester for 112 runs. The innings lasted for three hours until two o'clock when lunch was taken. Maldon's response lasted until half past five, when they were finally dismissed for 97 runs, shared mainly among Goodhew, Lawrence, James Page and Beale. In the remaining half an hour, Colchester made nine runs for two wickets before stumps were drawn at half past six.

By the time of the next reported match in 1862, Maldon had entered the 'Silcock era' when they were bolstered by the services of their best ever player. The stars of the Potman Marsh days had faded from the scene to be replaced by talented younger players under the capable and ambitious direction of Thomas Tomlinson. The club could now take on the best and regular matches with Colchester were played throughout the 1860s. Colchester too was strong, enhanced by the Owen brothers and the young James Round, then at Oxford University and destined to become captain of the Essex county club at Brentwood in 1876. Even so, they were unable to win this match, thanks to a slashing display by Brewster, Maldon's young number eleven, who hit 17 not out to pass Colchester's first innings total of 58. In fairness to Colchester, their second innings was standing at 102 runs for seven wickets when time was called and, as was the custom, the match awarded to Maldon on first innings.

In the return match at Maldon on 28 July, the home club completed a rare comprehensive victory in a two innings match that was played out. Although Colchester lacked some of their more eminent names, they had engaged the professional services of Foster, who took nine wickets in Maldon's first inning. See next page for the scorecard.

Another win, by four wickets, was recorded in 1863. Playing in the grounds of the Manor House at Lexden, Colchester again employed the professional, Foster, and included another guest, a Mr Hatcher. Maldon had recruited John Tabor of Bocking and John Ballard, a wicket-keeper from Burnham-on-Crouch, who later moved to Chelmsford and appeared for the Essex county club between 1876 and 1880. Colchester made 42 runs in their first innings and a formidable 95 runs in their second. Thanks to a stylish 40 runs from Tabor, however, Maldon totalled 113 runs in their first innings and, despite the

Maldon versus Colchester, at Maldon, 28 July 1862

Colchester	*First Innings*		*Second Innings*	
Almond	run out	8	b. Silcock	11
J. H. Hills	b. Silcock	13	c. Davis b. Gower	2
A. F. Hills	c. Going b. Gower	5	b. Silcock	6
Burney	b. Silcock	14	St. Page b. Silcock	2
T. Whale	lbw. Silcock	0	b. Silcock	0
Foster	b. Silcock	0	b. Gower	4
Capt. Raymond	Not out	13	Run out	1
Pettit	c. Ward b. Gower	2	c. Page b. Gower	9
Sainsbury	run out	2	b. Silcock	0
E. Cant	c. Davis b. Gower	0	b. Silcock	0
E. S. Daniel	b. Gower	0	Not out	0
Extras	byes 5, wides 4	9	byes 7	7
	Total	**66**		**42**

Maldon	*First Innings*		*Second Innings*	
H. Gower	b. Foster	8	b. E. Cant	3
Straight	b. Foster	5	b. Foster	2
Silcock	b. Foster	7	not out	16
R. Page	c. Sainsbury b. Foster	30		
Tomlinson	b. Foster	3	not out	13
Davis	b. Foster	4	b. Foster	0
Going	b. Foster	0		
James Page	b. Almond	1		
Ward	Not out	2		
Fuller	b. Foster	1		
Digby	c. & b. Foster	2		
Extras	byes 4	4	byes 8, wides 1	9
	Total	**67**	**(for 3 wickets)**	**43**

hostility of Foster, scraped together the 25 runs needed for victory, for the loss of six wickets.

On 28 May 1866, Maldon played the newly styled 'Colchester and Essex County Club' on the new ground that had been part of the army barracks off Wimpole Lane. To mark their newly acquired status, Colchester had engaged the 20-year-old professional, William Marten, for the season. Marten, a fast round-arm bowler, played first-class cricket for Kent and Surrey between 1865 and 1872 and was another player to represent the Essex county club in 1876. Marten duly took seven Maldon wickets in the first innings, but determined play by Henry Gower, John Ballard, Church and Copsey helped towards a total of 99 runs.

Maldon's professional, Frank Silcock, took eight wickets, with only Hills (32 runs) and Tabor (26 runs), making significant contributions towards Colchester's total of 75 runs. Batting again, Maldon made 46 runs in the second innings but were awarded the game when time was called with the Colchester team at 19 runs for two wickets in its second inning.

Maldon's dominance over the supposedly strongest club in the County continued with two easy victories in 1867. At the Fairfield, Silcock scored an undefeated 69 and Tomlinson 37, as Maldon set a huge score for the time of 167 runs. The visitors (now styled 'Colchester and East Essex') had scored 58 in the first innings, when Tomlinson's 'slows', tantalising underarm lobs, had captured eight wickets. Batting a second time, Colchester were four wickets down for 24 runs and well on the way to an innings defeat when the match ended and Maldon secured victory on first innings.

In the return match at Colchester, good batting throughout the order saw Maldon to a first innings total of 124. The strong Colchester team that included Francis Round could only respond with 52 runs in the first inning and 48 runs in the second. Maldon had won by an innings and 24 runs.

By the time of the last match of this series Maldon had lost the services of Frank Silcock, who made his debut for the Players against the Gentlemen in 1868, but the team under Tomlinson had matured and strengthened, with the likes of Charles Escott, another future Essex player, joining the club. Colchester was strong, fielding the same John Ballard who had previously appeared for Maldon and C. R. Stevens of Witham, another member of the early Essex county club at Brentwood. Maldon again proved too good:

Maldon versus Colchester, at Maldon, 4 July 1868

Maldon	*First innings*		*Colchester*	*First innings*	
C. H. S. Escott	b. Bray	13	Somerville	c. Page	6
T. Tomlinson	b. Sheo	3	C. Dyke	c. Tomlinson b. Self	0
R. C. Timperley	b. Bray	5	E. Sheo	c. Escott	3
H. Gower	b. Bray	0	Bray	st. Tomlinson	7
Jos. Beale	b. Sheo	18	E. Cant	b. Self	23
R. Page	b. Bray	12	C. R. Stevens	c. Jno. Beale	10
A. Self	b. Bray	38	J. Ballard	b. Chaplin	0
Jas. Page	b. Bray	1	H. Lyns	b. Tomlinson	11
C. Chaplin	not out	26	V. W. Taylor	c. Jas. Page	3
C. Brooke	b. Bray	1	E. Daniell	not out	7
John Beale	b. B. R. Cant	5	B. R. Cant	b. Self	2
Extras	b 3, l.b.3, w 1	11		B 4, l.b. 1, w 1	6
	Total	**133**			**78**

Maldon scored 17 runs for one wicket in the second innings and were awarded the match. Bowlers' names only are given for dismissals in the scorecard.

From the match reports that appeared in the *Chelmsford Chronicle* Maldon had an excellent record against Colchester, losing only an unfinished match in 1855 out of ten games played in 25 years. During this period, Maldon built its capable team from the days of Potman Marsh into a strong and respected one that increasingly looked towards London for its opposition. Paradoxically, when Maldon next met Colchester in 1872, it lost by 50 runs on first innings.

Chapter 10

Maldon versus Witham 1848–1858

Maldon had played two matches against Witham in 1828, but the series of games between the clubs in the decade after the move to the Fairfield was the most enjoyable and keenly contested on record. Witham were Maldon's nearest opponents of suitable standing, well matched in playing strength and progressive in outlook. Both clubs employed professionals when necessary and both produced cricketers who progressed to county level. Matches between them became an eagerly anticipated occasion in the cricket year.

When the series started in 1848 each club was undergoing something of a transformation. Maldon's move to the Fairfield had opened up bright future prospects, while Witham had appealed to the townsfolk for donations towards the club's expenses and the payment of professional players. The public interest so aroused resulted in substantial crowds at Mr Pattison's Witham ground on match days.

Maldon played the first match there on Monday, 10 July, 1848, losing on first innings by 19 runs. As the somewhat whimsical cricket correspondent of the *Chelmsford Chronicle* records, it was an unexpected result:

> In consequence of the reputation which the gentlemen of the Maldon club had gained as being 'Invincibles', it was generally expected that they would come off victorious and the apparent 'steam shot' bowling of Beckwith at the commencement of the game seemed to strengthen this opinion, but it was not long before the Witham

8. The Fairfield Maldon. Victorian serenity is captured in the scene of the Maldon club's new ground. The White Horse and the King's Head are among the buildings beyond the field.

> gentlemen discovered that if swift bowling when met with a straight hit, caused a dead stop, yet a leg or a slip hit would have the desired effect of sending the ball to its whereabouts without much fear of its breaking the stumps of the batsman, and the superior batting of Mr B. Cant, in this respect, gave ample proof of the correctness of this opinion.

This is a fine example of the wordiness of the nineteenth century journalist, who was presumably saying that Cant, alone of the Witham players, excelled at pulling and cutting the fast bowlers. Cant certainly rescued the game for Witham, as the scorecard shows (see next page).

The Maldon team for this match was a strong mixture of the seasoned stalwarts of Potman Marsh and the next generation of young cricketers. William and Richard Devenish, William Beckwith, John Rumsey and James Beale were all established players, while the up and coming Tomlinson, Bulley and Cooper added depth to the batting and variety to the bowling. For Witham, Gee and Isted (who was engaged periodically by Maldon) were professionals and the names of Cant and Nunn were very familiar in Colchester cricket circles.

Maldon versus Witham, played at Witham on Monday, 10 July 1848

Maldon	*First innings*		*Second innings*	
Beale	run out	6	c. Nunn	4
Tomlinson	b. Haines	8	b. Oscroft	9
Blanks	c. Oscroft	10	c. Nunn	13
Cooper	b. Oscroft	10	b. Haines	0
Bulley	b. Haines	0	c. W. Cant	3
W. Devenish	lbw.	1	b. Oscroft	0
Beckwith	st. Kirkham	1	b. Oscroft	6
R. Devenish	c. Nunn	7	b. Haines	7
Clarke	run out	0	b. Haines	8
W. Clarke	not out	0	b. Oscroft	2
Gepp	b. Oscroft	0	not out	4
Extras	byes 5, wides 2	7	byes 9, wides 2	11
	Total	**50**		**67**

Witham	*First Innings*		*Second Innings*
Coe	c. Cooper	4	
King	lbw.	0	
W. Cant	b. Beckwith	1	
Nunn	c. Beale	1	
Haines	c. Tomlinson	1	
B. Cant	b. Beale	22	
Gee	c. Tomlinson	9	
Oscroft	b. Beckwith	1	
Kirkham	not out	2	
C. King	b. Beckwith	0	
Dace	b. Beale	0	
Extras	byes 22, wides 6	28	
	Total	**69**	

Match awarded to Witham on first innings

During the next ten seasons, the Maldon and Witham clubs played 15 further matches, nearly half of the total of all Maldon's reported games during that period. Witham won one match outright and seven on first innings; Maldon won five on first innings and two games were drawn. For the first five years, neither club succeeded in beating the other home and away, but towards the end of the decade, Witham gradually established the superiority of their playing strength.

In 1849, Witham decided that the Maldon men were 'out and out teazers' rather than 'invincibles', a point they proved by taking the game by 25 runs on first innings. The victory was, however, overshadowed by Maldon's second innings score of 135 runs for five wickets against the professional bowling of Isted and Gee. The hospitality that followed the match was typical of the enjoyment gentlemen took from their cricket and underlined the camaraderie between the two clubs:

> In the evening a large party of friends and supporters of the club assembled at the Eagle Inn, and after partaking of the good things provided by the landlady, Mrs Nunn, several loyal and appropriate toasts were proposed and heartily responded to. The evening's entertainment was much enhanced by several fine glees and songs. On the whole the day passed off most pleasantly.

In the return match Maldon won by 25 runs on first innings, bowling Witham out for 45 and 67 runs thanks to Cooper, who took 13 wickets in the match. Time prevented Maldon from scoring a further 24 runs in the second innings needed for a comprehensive win. Such was the friendly rivalry between the clubs that a third and deciding game was suggested but arrangements were not completed.

Closely fought tussles continued into the 1850s and, after five years, neither club had completed home and away wins.

Higher scores began to be made, as in the drawn game in 1852, when Witham topped 200 runs in the first innings and Maldon responded with 78 runs for just two wickets. In 1853, the Du Cane brothers, Charles and Alfred, added their talents and prestige to the Witham club but, again, each club won one match on first innings.

Maldon, by contrast, was suffering a temporary decline as the powers of the stalwart players faded and they gradually disappeared from the cricket field. For the first match in 1856, the sole surviving name from the team that played Witham in 1848 was Thomas Tomlinson. The game was lost heavily and would have proved the first comprehensive victory for Witham had rain not terminated Maldon's second innings at 98 runs for eight wickets, when the scores in the match were exactly even. With an improved team Maldon returned the compliment in the return match at Witham, making 131 runs in the first innings and reducing Witham to 63 and 47 runs for seven wickets in its two innings.

The mutual respect between the clubs became strained towards the end of the series of matches, with comments both about the strength of the Maldon club and the condition of the Fairfield ground aired in the newspaper. Sensitive to their situation, the Maldon committee bought in two professionals, Moody and Payne, for the second match in 1857, after the first had provided Witham with its first comprehensive win by an innings and 80 runs. The professional pair enabled Maldon to achieve a face saving win on first innings, 143 runs to 115.

Finally, in 1858, Witham won both matches, proving their ascendancy over the declining fortunes of Maldon within the County cricket scene. At Witham in July, the home club scored freely to notch a first innings total of over 200 runs before dismissing Maldon for 146 runs. The scorecard for the return game at Maldon, where the Fairfield was described as 'not as good as might be expected' is shown in full on the next page.

Maldon versus Witham, played at Maldon on Friday, 16 July 1858

Witham	*First innings*		*Second innings*	
R. King	b. Payne	13	b. Payne	4
J. Isted	b. Payne	1	not out	7
A. Du Cane	b. Payne	28		
A.B. Fane	Run out	11		
E.S. Bowlby	b. Payne	0	not out	9
W. Pattisson	b. Payne	4		
H. Nunn	run out	13	c. Tomlinson b. Payne	20
A. Coe	b. Dyke	2		
W. King	b. Payne	4	b. Tomlinson	8
J. Pattisson	b. Dyke	0		
H. Butler	Not out	7		
Extras	b.15, l.b.5, w.5	25	b.6, l.b.2, w.5	13
	Total	**108**	With 3 wickets down	**61**

Maldon	*First innings*		*Second innings*
Young	b. Isted	4	
R. Blanks	c. Isted b. Pattisson	4	
R. Page	b. Isted	9	
R. Payne	c. Coe b. Pattisson	12	
T. Tomlinson	c. Butler b. Isted	3	
W. Clarke	b. Isted	3	
C. Dyke	b. Pattisson	3	
G. Hetherington	b. Isted	15	
H. Rush	b. Pattisson	0	
J. Page	b. Isted	2	
J. Rumsey	not out	2	
Extras	b.11, l.b.3, w.5	19	
	Total	**76**	

Over the decade, these matches show Witham, with the support of the townsfolk, developing a powerful cricket club. Professionals, Isted, Gee and then Carpenter, provided a bedrock of competence upon which fashionable talents like Cant and Nunn of Colchester – and later the Pattissons and Du Canes, could build. Increasingly high scoring as the decade progressed is evidence of improved pitches at Witham, while the quality of Maldon's Fairfield apparently declined.

After finally achieving the double over their old rivals, Witham stopped playing Maldon after 1858 and the match never appeared again as a regular contest until the 1980s. Maldon's period in the doldrums was, however, short lived and the club grew to prominence in the 1860s, under the influence of professional, Frank Silcock. Such was its reversal of fortunes that when it met Witham in a rare match in 1865, Maldon amassed 234 runs against Witham's 60 and 68 runs for four wickets.

Chapter 11
Maldon versus Tillingham 1861

When the Maldon club styled itself 'Amity' for the visit to Tillingham in 1861, it meant the team had been picked to provide friendly opposition against unproven opponents. Neither the captain, Tomlinson, nor the professional, Silcock, played in the team that consisted largely of occasional players and youngsters. The ploy backfired when Tillingham won the match easily.

Tillingham was not a village team in the 1860s, rather it was another venue used by the gentlemen of the Dengie peninsular. Dominated by the Pages from Down Hall, Bradwell, many of the same players appeared in sides variously called Bradwell, Southminster, Down Hall, Dengie Hundred – or Tillingham. Maldon players also appeared in these teams as, in 1868, when Tillingham were invited to play Mr Turner's Baddow Hall Eleven, more than half the side had also played for Maldon.

At this time, the major clubs had, at most, about ten organized games a season and these were played on any day of the week, except Saturday and Sunday. Gentlemen with leisure time available for cricket sought games wherever they could find them and the green in Tillingham village, opposite St Nicholas' church, provided a particularly attractive setting. The match on 21 August 1861, should not, therefore, be seen as a clash between town and village, but as a game arranged between the town and country factions of the Maldon club.

The green at Tillingham may have looked enticing for the first match in 1861, but the turf proved spiteful, as the *Chelmsford Chronicle* records:

> It will be remembered that the first game took place at Tillingham on August 21st, when the Tillingham gentlemen were victorious in one innings and several runs to spare. The Maldon gentlemen, attributing their defeat to the wretched state of the ground, made up their minds to meet their opponents (again) with the same eleven.

For the return match on Wednesday, 28 August, the Fairfield, 'under the able management of Frank Silcock' was 'in splendid order' and the weather was 'beautifully fine'. Maldon had not been able to keep the same side together for the return match because Wood and Barnard were unable to play. Clarke and Gill played in their place, but their inclusion would not have strengthened the side, from which players of the calibre of Tomlinson and Silcock were still omitted.

For Tillingham, the Pages and the Jacksons featured strongly, and 15-year-old Charles Escott, a future Essex player, appeared for the first time at the Fairfield ground that would become so familiar to him during his next 15 years. Tillingham won the toss and chose to bat against the opening bowling of 'Maldon's pets', Henry Gower and Jenner, 'neither of whom was as well on the spot as we have seen them'.

Despite their unaccustomed waywardness, resulting in a high quota of extras, the two youngsters, assisted by three run outs, dismissed Tillingham for 62, with James Page alone reaching double figures. When their turn came to bat, the pair made 42 of the 82 runs that Maldon scored in their first innings. Bowling again, Gower and Jenner – and two more run outs – had six Tillingham men out before James Page and James Jackson of Bradwell came together in a face-saving seventh wicket stand.

The *Chelmsford Chronicle* takes up the commentary:

> No stand could be made until Messrs. J. Jackson (Bradwell) and Jas. Page got together, who began to

> knock the ball about in all directions, when a change (of bowling) was deemed advisable and Mr Jackson was beautifully caught by Gower at long-field on in the second over of Ibbs, after adding 21 to the score. Mr Parker relieved Jenner and, in his second over found his way to Mr J. Page's wicket, who again contributed 11, comprising a beautiful leg hit for five, two twos and singles.

Tillingham scored 92 runs in the second innings, leaving Maldon to make 73 runs to win in the little time remaining. The young prodigies, Gower and Jenner, were sent in to bat against good bowling by Escott and Bradwell and, in attacking mood, they put 42 runs on the board to reaffirm the Maldon club's ascendancy. The match was awarded to Maldon on first innings. The full scorecard is given at the end of the chapter.

The match served to restore the goodwill between the players that seemed somewhat lacking after the first encounter at Tillingham. The cricket was good, with players of the future showing off their talents. Of Charles Escott, the newspaper commented, 'Mr Escott on the part of the Tillingham club is a very young player, and bids fair to become a fine bowler'. It was primarily as a batsman that Escott later came to Maldon and progressed to the ranks of the Essex county club when it formed at Brentwood in 1876.

The stars of the match were, however, the 'Maldon pets', Jenner and Henry Gower. For them, the *Chelmsford Chronicle* reserved the highest praise:

> We certainly must say they played beautifully, and should they be fortunate enough to get Frank Silcock for their tutor another year, in all probability they will be as useful men as any in the county.

Unfortunately, although Frank Silcock remained at Maldon for five seasons and Henry Gower became an integral part of the club for 20 years, Jenner's name disappears from reports after the 1862 season, although it did reappear briefly in 1867.

The match was completed in the time honoured fashion with drinking, eating and singing at the White Horse, where Mr Samms 'catered in his usual good style and everything passed off very pleasantly'.

Despite the happy ending of the day, further games did not take place between the clubs. It would be 100 years before Tillingham, as a strong village team, would beat the Maldon clubs of the 1960s.

Maldon versus Tillingham, played at the Fairfield, Wednesday, 28 August 1861

Tillingham	*First innings*		*Second innings*	
Jay	run out	4	c. & b. Gower	0
Jas. Jackson (Dengie)	b. Jenner	2	run out	5
Small	b. Gower	5	run out	8
C. Bradwell	Run out	0	b. Jenner	5
Robt. Page	lbw. Jenner	0	b. Jenner	8
Wm. Jackson	b. Jenner	6	st. Clarke b. Jenner	2
Jas. Page	c. Beale b. Jenner	11	b. Parker	11
Jas. Jackson (Bradwell)	run out	4	c. Gower b. Ibbs	21
Jas. Gale	b. Jenner	6	not out	8
Escott	c. Jenner b. Gower	0	b. Ibbs	2
Turner	not out	5	c. Gill b. Gower	5
Extras	b 11, w 7, nb 1	19	B 7, w5, nb 5	17
	Total	**62**		**92**

Continued on next page.

Maldon	*First innings*		*Second innings*	
Ibbs	c. & b. Bradwell	11		
Beale	Run out	2		
H. Gower	c. J. Page b. Bradwell	26	not out	14
Jenner	c. & b. Bradwell	16	not out	18
Clarke	b. Bradwell	11		
Parker	c. & b. W. Jackson	0		
Green	b. Bradwell	5		
Henderson	b. Bradwell	2		
Wm. Gill	b. Wm. Jackson	0		
Ward	Not out	0		
Horsnell	b. Wm. Jackson	0		
Extras	b 7, w 2	9	b 10	10
	Total	**82**	**with no wickets down**	**42**

Match won by Maldon on first innings.

Part 3

Victorian Players and Matches

Chapter 12

William Beckwith goes to Lords

William Beckwith was a Maldon man who played cricket for 20 years. He began his playing days on the rough surfaces of Potman Marsh but, by the time of his last games in 1854, the cricket club had moved to the more refined surroundings of the Fairfield that lay behind the fashionable top end of the High Street (the Upper Plume School site today). Beckwith was a fast bowler but his action was so controversial that protests from opponents forced Maldon to refer him to a panel at Lords.

Bowling styles had developed rapidly since the early days when the ball was literally bowled along the ground. By the time of Maldon's early matches in the 1770s underarm deliveries would be pitched to a length forcing changes to batting technique and the straightening of the bat blade. Then, in 1792, Tom Walker of the famous Hambledon club raised his bowling arm to shoulder level and sparked off a fierce debate about bowling actions that would rage for decades.

Although Walker's experiment was quickly declared unfair by the Hambledon authorities, who included most of the aristocratic patrons of the day, 'round arm' style attracted imitators who were less well disciplined by their clubs. The Marylebone Cricket Club (MCC) was in its infancy and had extreme difficulty regulating its own matches, and certainly had no influence over the conduct of cricket elsewhere. So for 30 years, the adjudication of fairness of bowling actions was left to umpires, heavily influenced by constant disputes with money backers and leading players.

Against this uncertain background the boy Beckwith grew up and developed his 'steam shot' bowling action that caused fright among unprotected batsmen on the rough saltings of Potman Marsh. By the time he started playing for the club, however, the MCC had begun to exercise authority over the game as a whole and, after overcoming last ditch conservative protests, round arm bowling was legalised in 1835. The problem was that, by then, bowlers had moved on even further and were experimenting with 'high round arm', or overarm, deliveries. It would take the legislators another 30 years of vacillation before the modern form of bowling was written into the laws.

The term 'steam shot' to describe Beckwith's action was coined by the *Chelmsford Chronicle* but could be misleading. At no time was a bowler allowed to throw or jerk the ball at the point of delivery, as seemed to be implied by the steam piston analogy. More likely, given that people of the time were marvelling at the power of early steam engines, the term is simply a tribute to the energy developed by Beckwith's low swing of the arm. But the gentlemen of the Chelmsford club thought otherwise.

Chelmsford in the 1840s was beginning to establish the primacy that it would later enjoy in the world of Essex cricket. It boasted many well-to-do members with county connections, men to be courted by clubs if they were to be accepted among the elite. It was unfortunate then that Beckwith also sometimes played for Dengie Hundred at Southminster, a club that Chelmsford would not play against, 'unless they give up their bowler, Beckwith'. A letter to the *Chelmsford Chronicle* from 'Long Stop', on behalf of 'ugly, awkward and troublesome customers' of the Dengie Hundred was an undisguised mockery of the self-regarding Chelmsford elite for their attitude towards Dengie and their fear of Beckwith. The Maldon cricket establishment must have been deeply concerned about the damage such indelicate publicity might do to their relationship with Chelmsford.

Other clubs, like Witham, found nothing to complain about in Beckwith's action, rather they admired his abilities as part of the Maldon team they dubbed 'Invincibles'. Nevertheless there was a whisper that Beckwith was a 'thrower' and the Maldon committee, with the highest aspirations for the club and the move to the Fairfield imminent, could not risk any stain on its reputation. They asked the MCC if they could send Beckwith to Lords to be scrutinised by an umpiring panel.

The Lords adjudication was published in the *Chelmsford Chronicle* on 26 May 1848:

> BECKWITH'S BOWLING. The right of bowling according to the custom adopted by Mr W. Beckwith of Maldon, having been disputed, an appeal has been made to Lords Cricket Ground, and the following is a copy of the judgement dated May 22nd 1848 –
>
> We, the undersigned, umpires and players of the Marylebone Club, having this day witnessed the bowling of Mr W. Beckwith, of Maldon, Essex, hereby declare that the peculiar manner in which he delivers the ball, is fair and legal.
>
> (Signed.) Caldecourt, Bailey, Clarke, Diver, Dakin, Hillyer. Lillywhite, Royston, Sewell and Dean.

The signatories were all professionals, most of them bowlers, engaged by the MCC and included some of the greatest cricketers of the Victorian era.

So the suspicions hanging over Beckwith were dispelled and, in 1850, Maldon played two games against Chelmsford. The first was undecided after Chelmsford struggled to a first innings total of 84 in four hours. The return match at the Fairfield was won by Chelmsford but, in a two innings match, only 187 runs were scored for the loss of 37 wickets. The peculiarity was that Beckwith took only one wicket in both contests, and that in the second innings of the match at the Fairfield, where conditions clearly favoured the bowlers. Was he kept out of the attack as a diplomatic move by Tomlinson, or was he perhaps using a modified action that was less than effective? Or maybe a simple combination of ageing limbs and bad luck affected his performance.

The move from underarm to round-arm to overarm bowling increased the risk of injury to batsmen on crude pitches. Body padding began to evolve with makeshift leg guards appearing in the late 1820s and padded gloves first used by Felix in 1837. Cork was used for padding in the 1840s and, at the Great Exhibition of 1851, Lillywhites offered pads stuffed with horsehair for sale at 25 shillings a pair (about £70 today).

As the leading players of the day began to pad up, so their local counterparts followed the fashion, rushing to the London stores for equipment to protect themselves from bruising encounters with the likes of William Beckwith. Old players ridiculed the innovation. Writing to the *Chelmsford Chronicle* in 1856 one such veteran decried the use of padding 'in defence of legs and hands' likening it to 'armouring of batsmen as if for combat'.

But pads and gloves were here to stay as illegal overarm bowling became more insistent and enforcement of fair play virtually broke down. Finally, in 1864 the legislators at Lords grudgingly accepted reality and changed the laws to allow overarm bowling. As the nineteenth century drew to a close all forms of the bowler's art were practised at the Fairfield. Tomlinson type 'slows', lobbed to a length, would survive until the 1920s, while medium pacers like Frank Silcock persisted with their customary round-arm. As always, it was left to the new generation of cricketers to complete the overarm revolution and pave the way for the modern game.

Chapter 13

Thomas Tomlinson, captain extraordinary

The architect of the Maldon club's success in the mid-Victorian period was town surgeon, Thomas Tomlinson. During a period of 45 years, from 1846 to 1890, he served the club as player, captain and administrator, occupying honorary positions as both secretary and treasurer at various times.

The name of Tomlinson first appears in match reports in the 1820s. J. Tomlinson played as an all-rounder against Fryerning in August, 1824, while he and T. Tomlinson (possibly Thomas' father) both played against Waltham in July 1826. Thomas was born in 1828 and privately educated to succeed his father as the town surgeon for Maldon.

The first game Thomas played for Maldon was in 1846 when he represented the Single Men against the Married Men on Potman Marsh. The following year, he played in a club match against Stock, making 38 runs out of a first innings total of 125. Maldon won the match easily on first innings, with Rumsey, Beale and Hurrell bowling out Stock for 84 runs. Tomlinson had the opportunity later in 1847 to demonstrate his own bowling skills in a game between under-21 teams of Maldon and Southminster. A large crowd watched the young gentlemen of Maldon demolish the visitors in 40 minutes for just 21 runs, before posting a total of 68 runs. Tomlinson added six wickets to the five he took in the first innings, as Maldon was given just 17 runs to win. Victory was duly secured but three wickets were lost in the process.

Tomlinson had grown up during a period of great turbulence in cricket that resulted in the legalisation of round arm bowling in 1835. He did not, however, practice the new style but adhered to the underarm method. 'Tomlinson slows', lobbed to a precise length, became notorious in the county and brought him a healthy harvest of wickets during the next 30 years. It is clear from his early performances that he was also a capable batsman, often filling the number three position in some of the best matches. Maybe he did not fulfil his potential and, under his own captaincy, he usually slipped towards the bottom of the order unless the batting was weak.

As a young man he joined a powerful side at Potman Marsh, playing alongside men like Dick and Will Devenish, the controversial fast bowler, Beckwith, Beale and Rumsey. These men were capable of humbling the best teams as they proved in 1844, when Writtle, then at the height of fashion, were thrashed by an innings and 40 runs, and Colchester, by 151 runs. They even managed a first innings win against Bishops Stortford, the pride of Hertfordshire.

But the potency of the Potman Marsh generation was beginning to fade and a new group of youngsters like Jenner and the Gowers, under the leadership of Tomlinson, would supplant it. The move to the new cricket ground at the Fairfield in 1848 was symbolic of the modernisation that the Maldon club underwent. Cricket was changing fast with bowlers' arms going higher and higher and batsmen responding, both in technical modification to their play and in wearing the new padded gloves and leg guards.

The greatest push towards the modern era came, however, from the invention of the lawn mower. The infertile saltings at Potman Marsh had been an ideal location for early cricket, requiring little preparation and providing an endless selection of pitches on which to play. The move to finer turf at the Fairfield and the use of a cylinder mower and cast-iron roller produced flatter surfaces on which to face the increasing pace and bounce of emerging overarm bowling.

Tomlinson was the man to lead the Maldon club into the modern era. From his debut in 1848 he missed only a handful of the reported matches until the late 1870s. The fortunes of the club dipped during the 1850s as the new generation replaced the old, but by the 1860s, with the employment of Frank Silcock as professional player, groundsman and coach, Maldon's future was secure. The Maldon club chose who they would play, frequently beat the best clubs in the County and travelled with increasing frequency to meet London clubs. The zenith of Maldon's fame came in the 1870s with visits to the Fairfield by the professionals of the All England Eleven, and by C. I. Thornton and his colourful amateurs of the Orleans club at Twickenham.

Tomlinson may have been a useful cricketer but it was probably his social gifts that served the Maldon club best. In the rigid class hierarchy of Victorian society cricketing ability and ground facilities counted for nothing unless they could be merged into a formula for social acceptability. Tomlinson, a well-educated professional man with sufficient wealth and leisure time, obviously communicated well with the sons of wealthy middle-class families, who gravitated naturally towards the cricket clubs at Colchester, Chelmsford and Witham. The country house matches at Down Hall, Bradwell, and Woodham Mortimer Place provided opportunities to mix with some of the leading lights of Essex cricket and Tomlinson was highly successful in forging lasting contacts with them. The result was that the standing of Maldon among the elite Victorian clubs was assured.

Another result was that Tomlinson received invitations to play in some important matches. He appeared for Charles Du Cane at the beautiful Braxted Park ground and he played a few games with Du Cane for the Gentlemen of Essex. On 23 and 24 August 1855, he played for Sixteen of South Essex against the United England Eleven at Upton Park. He made an undefeated second innings score of 13 runs, but the powerful United Eleven that included Grundy, Dean, Lockyer, Caffyn and Wisden, won the match by ten wickets. The game was played for the benefit of W. Goodhew, the professional who had been engaged occasionally by Maldon, and he took six of the ten England wickets to fall.

Tomlinson's priorities remained with the advancement of the Maldon club and, in 1859, he took a team to Upper Tooting to play in 'the charming grounds of T. J. Miller, Esq., Member of Parliament for Colchester'. The weather threatened to mar the sparkling social occasion but play was possible at one o' clock, when Mr Miller's Eleven proceeded to score 119 runs, the innings closing

> just as dinner was announced, when the players and a large party of private friends partook of an elegant collation at the invitation of the honourable member.

The several toasts after the meal did little for the Maldon team that was forced to follow on, having been dismissed for 58 runs. The second effort was a little better: the gentlemen totalled 90 runs when time was called at seven o'clock and the game was awarded to Miller on first innings.

The matches at the Page's family home at Down Hall, Bradwell, also became increasingly glittering occasions and, as the Tomlinson years passed, he took his own team to play an annual match against some of the brightest prospects on the Essex cricket scene. In 1870 a match at Lord Petre's exclusive venue at Thorndon Park was secured, when a modest Maldon team beat the assembled company of all stars.

As Tomlinson's connections in the world of cricket grew, so too did those with the great and the good of Maldon's citizens. By 1872 he had become a borough councillor and began taking a wider interest in the town's affairs. It was a happy coincidence that both his personal aspirations and those of the corporation were met by the cricket match against the All England Eleven in 1873. The travelling professionals were still a major visitor attraction and it was the expected influx of tourists and their money that sealed the support of the civic leaders.

In the event it was a fine cricket and civic occasion. Tomlinson captained the Maldon club to an historic victory and, but for the butter-fingers of Ollie Shore, the vicar of Langford, he would have had the wicket of Nottinghamshire's opener, Tom Bignall. Securing a match with the All England Eleven was simply a matter of guaranteeing the required money, so the visit by C. I. Thornton's Eleven in 1878 was the greater coup. Whatever the channels of influence were that brought some of the greatest players of the age at a day's notice from the Prince's ground in Middlesex to Maldon, Tomlinson's network must have played a part. To have 'Buns' Thornton (so called because he once took an outfield catch while eating a bun), 'Monkey' Hornby, 'the Demon' Spofforth and E. M. Grace all on display at the Fairfield is history indeed!

The 1878 match is also interesting because Tomlinson, though still captain, host and speechmaker, took little part in the play. He batted number eleven and did not bowl until the closing exhibition stages of the match. Then aged 50, it is reasonable to suppose that his physical capabilities were deserting him and thereafter his appearances for the Maldon club were less and less frequent.

He appears, however, to have clung onto the captaincy until 1890, by which time the club was in serious decline. The generation of players that had taken Maldon to prominence in the 1870s had retired from the game without being fully replaced. More importantly, the standing of the club in the decade when Essex cricket was preparing for first-class status was allowed to slip. Tomlinson, perhaps the greatest servant the Maldon club has ever had, held onto the reins until he was 62 years of age, when the enthusiasm and energy that he had so readily invested in his youth was difficult to muster.

With his going, the great days of cricket at the Fairfield also departed. It would be 100 years before Maldon would again compete against the best clubs in the region.

Chapter 14

Frank Silcock, Victorian professional

Frank Silcock, the bowling hero of the victory over the All England Eleven in 1873, was the best cricketer ever to play for Maldon. His contribution as the club's professional between 1861 and 1867 laid the foundations for the club's rise to prominence in the ensuing two decades.

He was born in Sawbridgeworth in 1838 and, by the age of 17, was playing for the powerful Bishops Stortford club. Here he came under the influence of his cousin Joe, a professional cricketer six years his senior, and formed a lifelong association with bowling legend, John Hughes. Both Joe Silcock and Hughes played numerous matches for and against Maldon in later years and it was, of course, Hughes who joined Frank Silcock in the rout of the All England Eleven at the Fairfield in 1873.

In his boyhood years Silcock learned the trade of saddler and harness maker but cricket was his passion and he was blessed with sufficient talent to embark upon a career as a professional player. He was tall and well built. He bowled traditional round arm at brisk pace and his stylish right-handed batting brought him many runs in the middle order of the teams he represented. The life of a professional cricketer in the 1850s was a precarious one with no structure of county clubs and only the very able few considered for membership of Clarke's All England Eleven, launched in 1846.

Silcock, therefore, hired his services to the wealthier clubs around the Essex and Hertfordshire borders, where the Maldon club first encountered him playing for Billericay in

9. Maldon's best ever cricketer. A relaxed Frank Silcock (standing second from the right) pictured with W. G.'s mighty United South of England Eleven in 1871. Ted Pooley stands in characteristic pose on the extreme left.

Others pictured are (standing) John Lillywhite, C. Griffith, T. Humphrey, James Lillywhite (junior), (sitting) H. Charlwood, G. F. Grace, W. G. Grace, J. Southerton, (on duckboard) H. Jupp and R. Humphrey.

August, 1860, with his cousin Joe. A large crowd of spectators attended the match, including many ladies, which doubtless made Maldon's annihilation at the hands of the Silcock cousins the more humiliating. Joe took six wickets and Frank four as Maldon were shot out for 26 runs, whereupon the Billericay innings of 120 runs was dominated by Frank's hard hit 80. Joe's eight wickets in the second innings consigned Maldon to an enormous defeat by an innings. The following year Frank Silcock came to Maldon to be the professional at the Fairfield.

As well as playing for the club, the professional was expected to act as groundsman and coach. Silcock excelled in all departments. Under his care the Fairfield became recognised as one of the finest grounds in the county and his influence over the development of young players was profound. Henry Gower, Charles Escott and the young bowler, Jenner, were particularly fortunate to have his tutelage during their formative years.

Although he settled in the town, helping to run the The Chequers inn until 1869, Maldon did not have the professional's exclusive services. In the 1860s there were only a handful of matches with other clubs each season and cricket was played throughout the week. After discharging his obligations to Maldon, Silcock was free to seek match fees wherever patronage could be found. The arrangement worked well for all parties as Silcock's growing reputation brought him – and Maldon – to the attention of the best clubs. Before long the two great patrons of Essex cricket, Lord Petre of Thorndon Hall and Lord Braybrook of Audley End were employing Silcock at their magnificent country house grounds.

This was the era of the aristocratic wandering clubs like I Zingari, Cambridge Quidnuncs and the Incogniti, whose talents were every bit as lavish as the hospitality that was poured out on match days. Although Silcock and his brother professionals were not allowed to eat in the same tent, his agreeable personality and cricketing ability brought him much respect from the company.

Maldon meanwhile, with Silcock's assistance, began to dominate matches against Colchester and to perform with increased panache against other opponents, including the officers of the Colchester Garrison and old adversaries, Witham and Stock. The clubs at Gosfield and Springfield emerged briefly onto the fashionable circuit but Maldon looked increasingly towards London, securing games against clubs like Islington Albion and Upton Amicables.

Silcock was invited to play at Lords against the MCC on 1 and 2 June 1863. He took three wickets in the first innings and scored three and 14 runs in a match won by the MCC by seven runs. The following year he secured a place in the United England Eleven (U.E.E.) (that had split from the All England Eleven in 1862), when some of their regular players were late returning from the Australian tour. He did not play regularly but was still engaged by the U.E.E. when Lillywhite and Willsher contrived the further breakaway by the south of England players. Unfortunately for Silcock, he was not engaged by the United South of England Eleven and he could not remain with the northern players who now comprised the U.E.E.

Instead, he began a long association with the public schools as a coach. In 1864 he was engaged by Uppingham School and by Felsted in the early summer of 1865. During the late summer he worked with the officers at Colchester barracks and later, between 1871 and 1874, he was at Eton. The principal job of the coach was, of course, to bowl at the 'young gentlemen', although by so doing he probably taught them more about batting than a host of theorists could today. It also helps to explain the phenomenal accuracy of the old professionals who were required to bowl for hour after hour to give practice to the aspiring batsmen of the age.

In 1866, Frank Silcock had a magnificent year, scoring 1278 runs in all matches for Maldon and others. He played in all the matches for the Essex county club that had formed at Colchester and hit 114 runs against Surrey Club in August. His abilities were at last recognised by the United South of England Eleven who invited him on the tour of northern England in September.

He was used as a number three batsman and occasional bowler against Eighteens of Manchester, Smethwick, Stockton and Bootle. All the games were dominated by foul weather that reduced grounds to swamps and, at Bootle, a hurricane blew the bails away. Silcock proved himself tough enough to perform with some credit and to keep his place in the side.

To celebrate the end of his breakthrough season, Silcock appeared with his Colchester colleague, Marten, and cousin,

Joe, for the Players of Essex against Twenty-two of Harlow. This was one of the closest matches on record at the time, finishing off the last ball of the game in a win for Harlow, for whom John Hughes had taken nine Essex wickets in the first innings and six in the second.

Silcock established his place in the United South of England Eleven and, for the next ten years, he took the field for and against the greatest players of the time. In the 1870s, the United South was dominated by the Grace brothers, including W. G., who Silcock had first met as an 18 year old in 1867, his last season at Maldon. Both men were chosen for 'England' against a combined Surrey and Sussex Eleven.

The following year Silcock was selected for the Players against the Gentlemen at Lords. Before there was any rational structure for choosing a national team, the highest achievement a cricketer could aspire to was to be picked for the annual clash between amateurs and professionals. The Gentlemen won the match by eight wickets but Silcock made the top score of 26 runs in the second innings, before he was bowled by W. G. Grace. He played again in 1869, making 49 and 40 runs in a high scoring match that the Gentlemen won by 17 runs. He also took five wickets in the match, including that of C. I. Thornton, who would bring teams to play at Maldon between 1878 and 1882.

In 1870, Frank Silcock began a four year stint with Hertfordshire, playing again alongside his cousin, Joe, and John Hughes. When the new Essex county club was launched at Brentwood under James Round in 1876, he was approaching 38 years of age, but soon became an established member of the team. In fact, he was so successful in the early years that his career with Essex lasted until 1893, despite being granted a benefit match in 1878, when he thought he would retire.

He continued to play under C. E. Green who masterminded the county's move to Leyton in 1886 that led to County Championship status in 1895. Finally, Silcock was given a second benefit match in 1893 and retired to run the cricket warehouse that he had established at Ongar some years earlier. He also stood as an umpire in county matches.

Frank Silcock, Maldon's best ever cricketer, did not enjoy a long retirement: he died at his Ongar home in May 1897, aged 58 years. The night before he died he awakened from a dream and asked for a favourite pair of cricket trousers that he put on with his cap and belt, declaring that he must prepare for a long journey.

Chapter 15
Charles Escott, Victorian amateur

C. H. S. Escott was another Maldon cricketer who featured in the victory over the All England Eleven in 1873 and went on to play for Essex when the county club formed at Brentwood in 1876. Unlike Frank Silcock, who had to take money from the game, Escott came from a privileged background and spent carefree summers with the fashionable set on the club and country house cricket circuits.

Escott was born in London on 27 May 1846. His father, a clergyman, brought his family to Tillingham in 1859, where he remained for 20 years as the incumbent of the parish of St Nicholas. The green and church lay together in the village centre and, doubtless, the teenage newcomer soon began to observe the Dengie gentlemen at play and to make the trek across the fields to Down Hall at Bradwell on match days.

The gentlemen of Maldon saw the young Escott's ability for themselves in the friendly games that were organized against Tillingham in 1861 (see Maldon versus Tillingham 1861 in Chapter 11). Although described as a 'promising young bowler', he had aspirations as a batsman and, by the following year, Escott was opening the innings for Tillingham, scoring 23 runs out of a total of 50 against Bradwell. More significantly, he had earned a place in Mr Page's Side at Down Hall in a match against Mr Tomlinson's Maldon Side.

Maldon included professionals, Silcock and Smart, while Page had brought in some of the best known amateurs in the County, such as Pattison of Witham, Cant of Colchester and the gifted Reverend Thackeray. Escott performed modestly in such company but his introduction to the top echelon of Essex cricket was made at the tender age of 16. He also began to learn the social graces as the large party of guests moved from the match to enjoy the generous hospitality always provided by the Pages.

In a powerful all round performance Escott top scored with 24 runs and took five wickets for Dengie Hundred in a rare defeat of Maldon. He was invited to become a member of the Maldon club and played his first game against Stock in 1862. Since the earliest days, Stock had been an important Essex club and matches with Maldon had been played periodically since the first encounter in 1771. On this occasion, the club was strengthened by professional, Joe Silcock, while his cousin, Frank, played for Maldon. Escott had an unspectacular debut, making nought and taking no wickets in a one innings match dominated by Frank Silcock and Henry Gower that Maldon won by 27 runs.

Although his name was to be found in various games around the Dengie peninsular, it was not until he had finished his education that Charles Escott became a regular member of the Maldon team. In 1867, at the age of 21, he played twice against Colchester in games that Maldon won, although his own contribution was not significant. Nevertheless, his potential must have been recognised and he was invited to play for the Colchester club in a two-day match against the celebrated wandering club, Incogniti.

He made yet another 'duck' in the first innings but scored 18 runs in the second innings and Colchester won the match by one run. Perhaps of more significance for Escott's future, he was playing alongside Francis Round and Charles Green, two giants of Essex cricket.

He met both Round and Green again when they came to play against Mr Page's Eleven at Down Hall, Bradwell, but he did not impress in that match. However, for Mr Ward's Eleven against Mr Clarke's Eleven at the Fairfield in 1867, he made an undefeated century – a very rare feat for the time. The *Chelmsford Chronicle* enthused, 'Mr Escott played a remarkably fine innings and the style in which he did it bids fair to do honour to Essex in the cricketing world.'

The prediction was sound. In 1868 he played for the Gentlemen of Essex and, the following year, he appeared in an Essex Eleven against Norfolk, performing well enough to establish himself among the elite of the county. In 1872 he travelled with 'Mr Usborne's team for Essex' to Ireland but played very little cricket during four days of continuous rain!

During this period he played in most of the Maldon games, as well as for Witham, Dengie and the many invitation matches that filled the summer calendar. In the All England Eleven match at the Fairfield in 1873, he made a valuable top score of 23 runs that held the second innings together and set a challenging total for the professionals to chase on the last day. When the new Essex county club formed under James Round at Brentwood in 1876, however, he moved his allegiance there.

On 13 and 14 June 1876, Escott participated in what is generally regarded as the first county match played by Essex. It was against Suffolk at Ipswich and Essex won by eight wickets, scoring 122 and 69 runs for two wickets, in response to Suffolk's totals 132 and 57 runs. Escott made an all too customary nought in the first innings and did not bat in the second, but he did open the bowling and dismissed both Suffolk openers.

Although James Round and Frank Silcock were both absent from this match, there were many playing colleagues who were familiar to Escott from his days at Maldon. Seth Smart (who played for Tomlinson at Down Hall) took seven wickets in the match and the former Colchester professional, William Marten, took eight. John Ballard, the wicketkeeper from Burnham-on-Crouch, had played for Maldon before moving to Chelmsford, and Charles Ridley was well-known among many of the elevens facing the Maldon club.

Against Hertfordshire at Bishops Stortford in July, a game Essex lost by an innings, Escott began to show some form with the bat and in the return match with Suffolk at Brentwood on 12 and 13 July 1876, he is credited with scoring the first half-century for Essex. During 1878, he made centuries against Colchester Garrison and the School of Gunnery at Shoeburyness, to seal his reputation.

In 1880, at the early age of 34, he stepped down from county cricket but continued to play for Brentwood until the turn of the century, when, at the age of 56, he could be found opening the batting against such clubs as Guy's Hospital. He also returned home sometimes to play for Tillingham & Bradwell (then combined), where a young H. G. Owen was beginning to make a name for himself. Owen became captain of Essex between 1895 and 1902 and was thus the first man to lead Essex in first-class cricket in the County Championship.

Escott also played with Owen's successor, C. J. Kortright, who many informed commentators reckoned to be the fastest bowler in the world until recent times. At the age of 18, Kortright took 79 wickets for Brentwood at an average of 6.4 runs apiece during the 1889 season. The Maldon club, then in slow decline, were unfortunate enough to meet Kortright that year, playing for Ingatestone. At the Fairfield, he scored 43 runs and took six wickets as Maldon were well beaten by 96 runs in a one innings match.

Charles Hay Sweet Escott led a bachelor life – he captained Brentwood's Single against the Married Men in an early season friendly in 1889 – that took him to the top of Essex cricket. He died, aged 74, at Brentwood on 11 August 1920.

Chapter 16
Gentlemen versus Players 1867

By 1867 the reputation of the Maldon club was approaching its height. The dip in fortunes that followed the retirement of the old Potman Marsh cricketers in the 1850s had been overcome by the engagement of Frank Silcock and the coming of age of the new generation of players. In strength and prestige the gentlemen of Maldon measured themselves against the best in the County, beating Colchester & East Essex by an innings on their own ground and winning against the officers of Colchester Garrison at the Fairfield.

Some of the most powerful teams were, however, encountered in the country house matches that increasingly absorbed the Maldon members. Leading cricketers and patrons would come to Down Hall and Woodham Mortimer Place, where Maldon's ambitious captain, Thomas Tomlinson, and his trusted henchmen took opportunities to forge links across the social divides. Their success in mixing with the leading lights of Essex cricket was celebrated towards the end of the 1867 season by a match styled, 'The Gentlemen versus The Players'.

In the days before a properly selected national team, a cricketer's highest achievement was to play in the Gentlemen and Players match at Lords. Looking back, the division of the world of cricket into privileged amateurs and humble professionals is seen as a crude reinforcement of an unacceptable Victorian class system. Fuller Pilch, the Bury St Edmunds player who became the greatest batsman of his time, recalled how the system worked at country house matches. After the day's play, the gentlemen and their guests would dine in the great hall while he, a professional cricketer, would take his supper in the kitchen. But, the young gentlemen would come downstairs at the first opportunity to smoke, drink beer and talk cricket at his table.

A typical gentleman of the time was James Round, who had represented Eton against Harrow at Lords in 1860 and, in 1867, had appeared there for the Gentlemen against the Players in a team that included the Grace brothers and the Walkers of Southgate. He became a barrister and Member of Parliament and the force behind Essex cricket in its early years and was, perhaps, the most illustrious name to appear in the match at Maldon.

Two other young amateurs who would play under Round in the Essex teams of 1876 appeared in the match, Charles Escott and C. E. Ridley. Escott was by then a regular Maldon player and Ridley could be found playing for several fashionable clubs, as well as for Uppingham Rovers (the old boys of Uppingham School where Frank Silcock began coaching in 1864). Others well-known on the local circuit were B. R. Cant of Colchester and Witham, J. E. Tabor of Bocking and the Taylors.

Robert Page, the farmer from Down Hall, Bradwell, brought his Dengie Hundred colleagues, Chillingworth and Kemp, and of the other Maldon members, Tomlinson, Timperley, Self and Jenner were classed as gentlemen, presumably because they had other recognised professions. Tomlinson was the town surgeon, Timperley the workhouse master and Self was the office manager at the thriving timber wharves of John Sadd & Sons.

Henry Gower, on the other hand was a boot and toy maker and hence classed as a professional, along with other Maldon regulars, Dyke and Sewell, who were presumably also tradesmen. There is no doubt about the status of Frank Silcock and his cousin, Joe: they were professionals of high reputation in Hertfordshire and Essex and had both played at Lords. For this match, Frank's brother, Fred, came to Maldon on one of the few occasions when all three Silcocks appeared in the same game.

The match, in which the Gentlemen's team was allowed 16 players was staged over two days, Tuesday and Wednesday, in August, 1867. The organization and expenses of such a match would have been considerable, involving lunches, dinners and overnight accommodation for everyone not living locally, as well as ground preparation and catering. It is possible that separate hotels, the Blue Boar and the King's Head, would have been used to give some of the visiting gentlemen the privacy and attention of their station in life.

The Gentlemen, batting first, sent in Escott, with a recent undefeated century to his name, and Ridley, but Frank Silcock quickly removed them both. Not until Page, Tabor and Cant demonstrated some middle order resistance did the Gentlemen show any authority but, after their departure, and in the absence of James Round, the innings crumbled to a total of 88 runs, thanks to 15 extras. Frank Silcock took seven wickets and Joe four, with Chapman claiming two victims.

The Players accumulated a total of just 49 runs, with the Silcock trio contributing just five runs between them. Only Henry Gower, batting at number ten, managed to reach double figures on a day when the ball dominated the bat. Charles Escott, who had originally been spotted as a bowler, proved he had not lost his all round talents with a haul of seven wickets. Alfred Self claimed the other three.

Robert Page topped the list of scorers with 30 runs in the second innings, with Round, having arrived late, making 17. Tomlinson also scored 17 runs in a significant innings total of 114. It was Joe Silcock's turn to take seven wickets with Frank and Smart sharing the others that fell.

Needing 145 runs to win, the Players never mounted a serious challenge. Hopes may have risen while Church (21 not out) and Frank Silcock (17) were together but they were short lived as Self took seven more wickets and the innings closed for 68 runs, leaving the Gentlemen victors by 85 runs.

The match attracted little newspaper comment and no further games between the teams were reported in subsequent years.

Gentlemen of Maldon versus the Players: a two-day match at the Fairfield played in August 1867

The Gentlemen	*First Innings*			*Second Innings*		
C. H. S. Escott		b. F. Silcock	2	c. J. Silcock	b. F. Silcock	8
C. E. Ridley	c. Fd. Silcock	b. F. Silcock	8	lbw.	b. J. Silcock	5
T. Tomlinson	c. Fd. Silcock	b. F. Silcock	1	c. Burrows	b. F.Silcock	17
A. Self	run out		8	c. & b.	J. Silcock	4
P. W. Taylor	c. Burrows	b. F. Silcock	0	c. H. Gower		0
J. Chillingworth	lbw.	b. Chapman	5	Run out		0
R. Page	c. Simpson	b. Chapman	10	c. Simpson	b. J. Silcock	30
J. E. Tabor		b. J. Silcock	14	c. Simpson	b. J. Silcock	1
B. R. Cant		b. J. Silcock	13		b. Smart	7
E. O. Jenner		b. F. Silcock	4	c. Fd Silcock	b. F. Silcock	2
C. R. Timperley	lbw.	b. F. Silcock	2	St. F Silcock	b. J. Silcock	0
T. A. Pearson		b. J. Silcock	1		b. J. Silcock	3
V. W. Taylor	c. & b.	F. Silcock	3	Hit wicket		1
J. Wiseman		b. J. Silcock	2	Not out		1
F. Kemp	Not out		0		b. J. Silcock	0
J. Round	Absent		0		b. Smart	17
Extras	b.9, l.b.4, w.2		15	b.14, l.b.4		18
		Total	**88**		**Total**	**114**

The Players						
W. Church		b. Escott	2	Not out		21
W. Burrows	c. Page	b. Self	9		b. Self	0
Fred. Silcock		b. Escott	3		b. Escott	1
Frank Silcock		b. Self	2		b. Self	17
F. Simpson		b. Escott	8	c. Jenner	b. Self	1
Joe Silcock	c. Chil.worth	b. Self	0	c. Jenner	b. Self	8
C. Dyke	c. Pearson	b. Escott	1	Run out		0
S. Smart		b. Escott	1	c. V. Taylor	b. Self	6
M. Chapman	lbw.	b. Escott	0	St. Round	b. Self	0
H. Gower	Not out		13	St. Round	b. Self	0
W. Sewell		b. Escott	2	Run out		5
Extras	b.8		8	b.8, w.1		9
		Total	**49**			**68**

The Gentlemen of Maldon won by 85 runs.

Perhaps the match was arranged partly to demonstrate Maldon's standing in the world of Essex cricket, and partly in tribute to Frank Silcock, who had reached the end of his six years as a professional at the Fairfield.

He was ready to move into the highest echelons of the Victorian game, leaving the Maldon club in an unprecedented state of good health. He would return for the epic match against the All England Eleven in 1873, but the gentlemen of Maldon would see more of him as an opponent in the ranks of such clubs as Ongar, Wanganui and Lord Petre's Thorndon Park Eleven.

Chapter 17
The All England Eleven 1873

The climax of the Maldon club's rise to prominence in Victorian times came when it defeated the professional All England Eleven in August 1873. The *Chelmsford Chronicle* boasted that the club could claim 'first place in the county' and that it was 'never in a more prosperous condition, better supported, and embracing more efficient players' than it was in 1873.

Yet it would be naïve to suppose that any club team could defeat professional opposition on level terms, even if that opposition was 'very weak, and contained several that had seen their best days', as the All England Eleven at Maldon was described in *Scores and Biographies*. The travelling elevens were in decline by the mid-1860s and attracting widespread criticism for their mercenary attitudes and below par performances. James Pycroft in *Cricketana* accused the professionals of being more interested in the sixpences taken at the gate than the runs they scored, and suggested their poor performances were because 'they are fagged and jaded – stale and overdone from the beginning of the season to the end'.

When the first All England Eleven was formed by William Clarke at the end of the 1846 season, all the great professionals gave their support because it promised them a regular income. Previously they had had to rely on whatever money they could earn from the promoters of early county games, the MCC and the wealthier clubs, schools and colleges. Clarke's proposals for a programme of up to 30 games a year, travelling the length and breadth of the country, created the prospect of five months of full time cricket and potential income of £180 a year for the professionals engaged.

Although the £5 or £6 match fee in the early days was attractive, it was not long before some of the players began to resent Clarke's profiteering from the gate money. In 1862, John Wisden and James Dean led a breakaway of the professionals of the south and formed the rival United All England Eleven. More factions split away in the years that followed with New All England Elevens being launched in 1858, 1861 and 1862 and the United South of England Eleven was formed in 1865, following an initiative led by John Lillywhite and Edgar Willsher.

By the 1870s, therefore, the strength of the professionals was dissipated across as many as four supposed England elevens, and their services were increasingly demanded for the growing number of county matches, as well as for national teams that the MCC was beginning to control. The gentlemen of Maldon were unconcerned about the deteriorating reputation of the All England Eleven. They thought a match would attract people to the town and show off the high standing of its cricket club – and they were right. A second initiative, also intended to bring huge numbers of visitors into the town in 1873, was to host the prestigious annual show of the Essex Agricultural Society.

The ideas came from prominent burghers of the town. The cricket challenge was proposed by the upwardly mobile draper, William Humpherys, at the cricket dinner in October 1872, and supported by wine merchant, Henry Sprague, who 'guaranteed that there should be no want of funds to meet the expenses'. A committee, consisting of Messrs. Tomlinson, Self, Copsey, Timperley, Moffatt, Sadler, Bridge, Brooke and Joseph, James and John Beale, was appointed to handle the arrangements and a subscription list of leading men of business was drawn up. An approach was made to the secretary of the All England Eleven, William Oscroft, and the organizing committee was overjoyed when the Eleven agreed to a match on 21

10. Champion professionals. Five of the professionals who played at Maldon for the All England Eleven are pictured with the 1875 Nottinghamshire team that won the county championship six times in eight years.

The team is, standing: (left to right) W. Shrewsbury, S. Biddulph, T. Nixon (umpire), M. McIntyre, R. Daft, J. West (umpire), J. C. Shaw, W. Oscroft. Seated: A. Shaw, J. Selby, F. Wild (on ground) F. Morley, A. Shrewsbury.

July, just a month after the Essex Agricultural Show was to be held. Subscriptions had brought in more than £90 and, in anticipation of large numbers of visitors, an agreement had been reached with Eastern Counties Railway to charge single fares for return journeys in first, second and third class carriages.

In the event, the match was postponed because a number of players, being professionals engaged by Nottinghamshire, had to give preference to a game against Surrey at the Oval that started on 21 July. Nottinghamshire won that match by 119 runs and six of the team, Bignall, McIntyre, Morley, Oscroft, Shaw and Wild, came to play at Maldon the following month. The 'several who had seen their best days' were Carpenter, Daniel and Thomas Hayward, Plumb and Tinley, but they had been great players in their time.

11. Thomas Hayward and Robert Carpenter. They may have 'seen their best days' by the time they played at Maldon, but Hayward and Carpenter had been among the best players in England.

Carpenter and Thomas Hayward played for Cambridgeshire when that county was among the strongest and, in the words of Richard Daft, they, 'astonished the whole of the cricket world for years after with their brilliant performances with the bat' for their county, the All England and the United England Elevens. Both men went with George Parr's tours to North America in 1859 and to Australia in 1863/64, being joined on the latter voyage by Tinley, who also played for Nottinghamshire between 1847 and 1869. Daniel Hayward played 31 times for Cambridgeshire and once – under the mistaken impression he was born in Mitcham – for Surrey. Plumb, the wicket-keeper, was 40 years old but would remain active for Northamptonshire for another eleven years.

Maldon was allowed 18 men to balance the odds. This in itself was a compliment as Southend in 1865 and Chelmsford in 1868 had each been allowed 22, with two given professionals. Maldon though engaged its own professionals, recalling former club man, Frank Silcock, who brought along his old mentor from Bishops Stortford and Hertfordshire, John Hughes. Hughes, at 48 years of age, was still reckoned to be one of England's finest bowlers, as his nine wickets for 82 runs off 47 overs against the MCC earlier in 1873 would seem to demonstrate. He would continue to ply his left-handed round arm bowling for another five years at first-class level, before reverting to professional for Bishops Stortford.

The remainder of the team is a tribute to Maldon's standing in the Essex cricket community, with the cream of its talent coming from clubs across the county. Thompson and Stevens, both future county players, came from Colchester, together with the Owen brothers. Wheeler came from London, and Isherwood was down from Oxford where he had earned a blue in 1872. From its own ranks Maldon fielded cricketers of the calibre of Escott, Henry Gower, Self, Sewell and Timperley and, of course, the captain, Thomas Tomlinson.

The organizing committee had paid every attention to detail. The Fairfield, 'at all times one of the most commanding (grounds) in the county' had received special grooming and 'the portion of the ground on which the wickets were pitched had been selected at the early part of the season, and had been most jealously guarded'. Canvass, surmounted by flags stretched across the top end of the ground, while tents and marquees furnished colour to the lower end. Bunting fluttered all around the ground and a dais for the town band had been erected. Mr Bridge had brought in a printing press and intended to issue a scorecard at the fall of each wicket, and Mr Revett of the King's Head had a well stocked licensed bar.

Carriage parking areas had been allocated and entry points carefully regulated to collect the sixpences from spectators. By Sunday evening all stood ready for the great match but during the night the rain began to fall.

Monday, 11 August

The overnight rain continued intermittently through the morning. Few spectators arrived and three of the Eleven's men were also missing. All the Nottinghamshire players had been involved in a win over Sussex at Trent Bridge that had finished a day early, but Oscroft and McIntyre had stayed to play in a single wicket match that was arranged at short notice to fill the Saturday. Carpenter had been playing at Grimsby for an All England Eleven and the three men had either been diverted by the delights of big town nightlife, or had miscalculated the difficulties of rail travel on Sundays.

The rain eventually cleared and play was possible at one o'clock. Tomlinson won the toss and chose to bat against the bowling of Shaw and Morley on a sodden pitch. The second ball of the mach from Shaw hurt Owen and in the fourth over, Escott was out without a run on the board. The professionals then demonstrated the art of fast bowling, sending down 14 overs at a cost of just four runs, but the pitch was too soft to make them dangerous.

Morley, just 23 years old, would become the first bowler to take 100 first-class wickets in a season in 1878, but Shaw, 37 years of age, was reaching the end of a distinguished career. Both men bowled left-handed at fast pace, Shaw in the old round arm style, keeping the ball hidden behind his back until the last moment, and Morley with a more modern high arm. They employed identical field settings with only two attacking short-legs on the on-side and seven men to the off. With only six fielders at the Fairfield (it is unknown whether substitutes[1] were given), they probably dispensed with one of the short-legs, cover point forward and mid-off.

After 20 four-ball overs, it began to rain again and lunch was taken with the score at 19 runs for three wickets. Mr Revett's hospitality in the large marquee was 'in very best style'.

Carpenter arrived on the three o'clock train and immediately took up his customary fielding position at point. The sun came out, the crowd began to grow and 'several carriages, glittering with the gay dresses of the ladies, drove onto the ground'. Shaw and Morley toiled away, Alfred Self played well and, when Owen was seventh out with the score at 59 runs, he was loudly cheered. He had struck four 3s, six 2s and seven singles[2] in a major score of 33, setting up a good total of 102 runs that was achieved by about half past five.

In the last 15 minutes of the day, Tomlinson decided to employ his 'slows' but was frustrated when Reverend Shore, the vicar of Langford, dropped Bignall at square leg. At the top end, Frank Silcock had bowled Plumb and the day finished at six o'clock with Bignall not out 5, and Wild not out 3. In the

---

1. Substitutes had been allowed under the laws since the 1820s, but not in the key fielding positions of wicketkeeper, long stop, point or cover point. By 1873, the consent of opposing captains was required as to fielding positions of substitutes, but it is not clear what the practice was when playing against professional elevens.

2. Boundaries were not written into the laws until 1884, but local conventions applied. In this match the ball was hit out of the ground for (presumably) a boundary six, and onto the scorer's tent for a boundary four. But for a ball that was struck into the crowd three runs were completed.

evening, 'the gentlemen[3] players sat down to an excellent dinner served by Mr W. Hickford of the Blue Boar hotel'.

Tuesday, 12 August

The second day brought everything the organizers had wished for. Bright sunshine was freshened by a friendly breeze, Oscroft and McIntyre had arrived and there was a 'thick cordon of spectators standing and sitting all around the ground' to listen to the Band of the Twenty-third Essex Reserve Volunteer under the direction of Mr Allen.

At twelve noon, Frank Silcock at the top end, and John Hughes began their demolition of the Eleven. Bignall added a single to his overnight score and, in the twentieth over from Silcock, 'Wild, striking at a ball, it flew from his bat, struck him violently on the face and knocked him down'. He continued, but not for long, when he was bowled by a shooter with the score on 21 runs. The pitch was drying under the hot sun and Silcock and Hughes were close to unplayable. Veterans Carpenter and Tom Hayward came and went, scoring a single between them, and McIntyre's lively innings was cut short when he was run out for seven.

Only Oscroft, a class batsman who represented Nottinghamshire for 18 seasons and toured Australia in 1873/74, defied the bowling, 'exhibiting beautiful defence', to be ninth out with the score at 36 runs. Jemmie Shaw dubbed by his Nottinghamshire captain, Richard Daft, to be 'the worst man with a bat that I ever came into contact with', was bowled first ball by Hughes. The All England Eleven had made just 36 off 169 balls, with Silcock taking five wickets and Hughes three. There were no extras: a tribute not only to the accuracy of the

3. It is unlikely that 'the gentlemen' included the professional players who likely supped at the King's Head and doubtless enjoyed their own company much more than that of the self-important Maldon subscribers.

bowlers but to the wicket keeping of Kemp and the athletic long stopping of Henry Gower.

Maldon, with a first innings lead of 66 runs, opened their second innings with Isherwood and Wheeler, who hit Morley on to the scorer's tent at square leg, in a bright innings that ended with the score at 28 runs for two wickets. When Kemp followed almost immediately for a duck, the players joined a large company for Mr Revett's lunch in the marquee.

The spite must have gone out of the turf in the afternoon as C. Sewell drove into the crowd for three runs and then hoisted Morley out of the ground, 'directly over a carriage situated in Mr Waring's front garden', for six. The backbone to the innings had been provided by Charles Escott but Stevens, a young batsman for both Colchester and Witham, played an inning of 19 that was 'greatly admired'. W. Sewell contributed a useful dozen and the Maldon innings terminated at close of play on 124 runs. Morley's professional persistence had earned him 13 wickets to add to the eight wickets he took in the first innings, at a total cost of 99 runs.

The crowd buzzed with anticipation as it dispersed to the various hostelries of the town. A total of 191 runs on a pitch that was now favouring the batsmen was well within the compass of the Eleven with the whole of the third day to bat. What a prospect to see some of the greatest players of their age contesting such a fourth innings against the skills of Maldon's famous bowlers and fine fielding. But as they wined and dined, the storm clouds gathered and the night rain again soaked the festive Fairfield.

Wednesday, 13 August

The Eleven never stood a chance under the hot sun that shone all morning to produce lethal bowling conditions by the time play started at noon. Morley was promoted to open the batting in front of another large crowd but went for nought after six maiden overs had been bowled. Bignall and Wild struggled manfully for a while but the score stood at 16 runs for three wickets after their departure. Oscroft again demonstrated the skills to survive but watched McIntyre, Carpenter and Tom Hayward depart at the other end, before he himself succumbed to another Silcock shooter when the score was 48 runs for seven wickets, and lunch was taken.

Poor Bullock, another occasional Colchester man, who had been 'floored' during the morning's play by a leg hit by Carpenter, must have had a painful lunch. When Carpenter was out, he was caught by a substitute, Wright, who had probably replaced the injured Bullock in the field.

Silcock and Hughes finished the task after lunch dismissing the Eleven for 58 runs. The only remarkable feature of the play being an innings of six by Shaw, who Daft insisted, 'was never worth four runs against any bowling in his life'! Silcock had taken six wickets for 20 runs (11 for 37 in the match) and Hughes four wickets for 32 runs (seven for 44 in the match). Between them they had bowled 101 four-ball overs and confirmed their reputation as two of the best cricketers in England.

The Nottinghamshire men left Maldon to travel to Hove where, the next day, they bowled the hapless Sussex side out for 19 runs. The innings was one of the lowest on record for a county match and lasted only 50 minutes, ending before Henry Phillips, the Sussex middle order batsman had arrived. He was recorded, 'absent (missed the train)'!

The Maldon organizers were cock-a-hoop. Their primary objective of bringing the town to the forefront of public attention had succeeded unreservedly and the cricket club had received an enormous boost to its prestige. Although the epic victory was down to Silcock and Hughes, at least they had connections with the club, and Maldon's own cricketers had contributed every bit as significantly as the distinguished guest players from around the County.

Over the three days of the match around 2200 members of the general public paid their sixpences at the gate to see the game, more than 1300 attracted by the fine weather on the Tuesday. In addition to them, three-day tickets were available for sale in advance and subscribers and their guests were, of course, entitled to free entry. Carriages to the ground paid a total of £5 to park. Although the All England professionals may not have been satisfied with their performance, the gate money would have been a great compensation for them.

But it was they that attracted the crowds to the inns and shops of the town and wrote a very important page in the history of the gentlemen cricketers of Maldon.

Eighteen of Maldon versus the All England Eleven: played at the Fairfield on 11, 12 and 13 August 1873

Maldon	*First Innings*			*Second Innings*		
C. Escott	c. Plumb	b. Morley	0	lbw.	b. McIntyre	23
J. Owen	lbw.	b. Morley	33		b. Morley	9
F. Silcock		b. Morley	3		b. McIntyre	0
F. Isherwood	c. Hayward	b. Shaw	0		b. Morley	4
H. Bullock		b. Shaw	0		b. Morley	7
A. Wheeler		b. Shaw	4		b. Morley	15
A. Self		b. Morley	11		b. Morley	0
C. Timperley		b. Tinley	9	st. Plumb	b. Shaw	5
C. Sewell	st. Plumb	b. Shaw	12		b. McIntyre	12
S. F. Kemp		b. Shaw	8		b. Morley	0
O. B. Shore		b. Morley	5	c. Tinley	b. Morley	1
C. R. Stevens	st. Plumb	b. Morley	0	c. Tinley	b. Morley	19
H. Gower		b. Morley	1		b. Morley	4
L. S. Owen	c. Tinley	b. Morley	4	c. D. Hayward	b. Morley	0
W. Sewell	c. Plumb	b. Shaw	0	c. Plumb	b. Morley	12
C. H. Thompson		b. Shaw	2	hit wicket	b. Morley	3
J. Hughes	not out		2	not out		0
T. Tomlinson		b. Morley	7		b. Morley	0
Extras	l.b.1		1	b.5, l.b.5		10
	Total		**102**			**124**

Bowling	Shaw	140 balls	51 runs	68 balls	16 runs
	Morley	155 balls	42 runs	174 balls	57 runs
	Tinley	20 balls	9 runs		
	McIntyre			104 balls	41 runs

The Eleven	*First Innings*			*Second Innings*		
T. Plumb		b. Silcock	0	not out		6
T. Bignall		b. Hughes	6	c. W. Sewell	b. Hughes	5
F. Wild		b. Silcock	10		b. Hughes	7
W. Oscroft	c. Silcock	b. Hughes	10		b. Silcock	15
R. Carpenter		run out	0	c. substitute	b. Silcock	3
T. Hayward	c. Kemp	b. Silcock	1	st. Kemp	b. Silcock	0
M. McIntyre		run out	7		b. Hughes	7
D. Hayward	c. Hughes	b. Silcock	0	c. Self	b. Hughes	2
R. C. Tinley	c. J. Owen	b. Silcock	0	c. L. S. Owen	b. Silcock	4
F. Morley	not out		2	c. L. S. Owen	b. Silcock	0
J. C. Shaw		b. Hughes	0	c. Self	b. Silcock	3
Extras			0	b.6		6
	Total		**36**			**58**

Bowling	Silcock	88 balls	17 runs	128 balls	20 runs
	Tomlinson	16 balls	7 runs		
	Hughes	65 balls	12 runs	124 balls	32 runs

Umpires: Ballard and Beale.

Maldon won by 132 runs.

Chapter 18

C. I. Thornton's Eleven 1878

Five years after the epic victory over the All England Eleven, some more of the most famous cricketers of the Victorian era were on display at the Fairfield. C. I. Thornton brought down a team of distinguished amateurs that included E. M. Grace, A. N. Hornby and F. R. Spofforth. On this occasion the club could not match the brilliance of the visitors, losing the one day match by an innings and 30 runs.

Thornton is perhaps not remembered as well as some of his contemporaries, but he was a legend at the time and remains one of the biggest hitters the game has known. He was typical of the carefree amateur produced by the public school and university system (Eton and Cambridge in his case), usually setting aside dour technicalities in favour of free and powerful hitting. By the age of 17 he was playing for Kent, and later appeared for Middlesex as well as Cambridge University. One of his historic big hits came at Canterbury, where he drove the ball 152 yards and, at the Scarborough festival, of which he was an early impresario, he hit the ball into neighbouring Trafalgar Square during an innings of 107 not out that contained 7 more sixes and 12 fours.

E. M. Grace, W. G.'s elder brother, also liked to hit the ball, often shamelessly across the line. He favoured the draw stroke, made by lifting the back leg and gliding the ball under it, and some say he invented the reverse sweep. He bowled fast round arm but later switched to underarm with which he took 119 wickets in club cricket in 1909, at the age of 68. Although overshadowed by his younger brother, E. M. Grace was a prodigious talent who played 253 times for Gloucestershire, toured Australia in 1863/64 and played in one official test match in 1880.

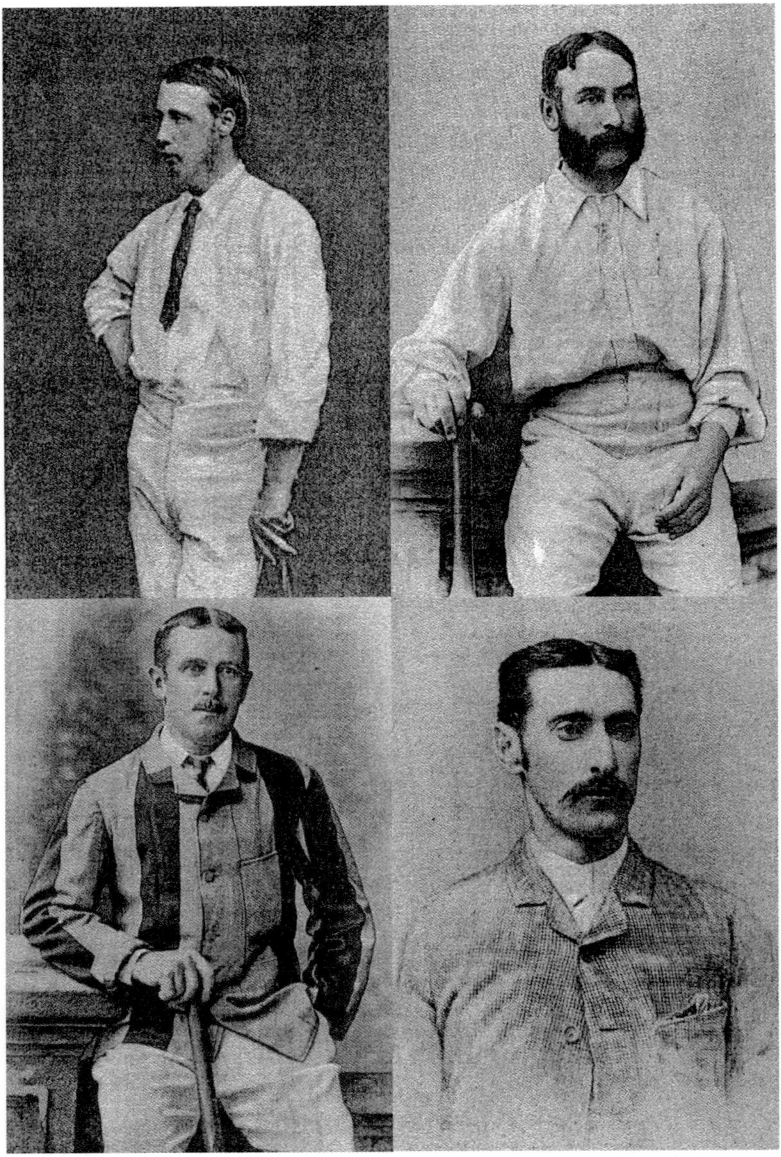

12. No greater players of the age. C. I. Thornton brought E. M. Grace, A. N. Hornby and F. R. Spofforth to the Fairfield in 1878.

Hornby, nicknamed 'Monkey' on account of his loping, muscular movements, was amongst the best batsmen in England. He was a right-handed opening batsman but bowled with either right or left hand. He played for Lancashire between 1867 and 1899 and was captain for 14 seasons, later becoming president of the club until 1916. Hornby played three times for England in official tests and was captain in 1882 when 'the demon' Spofforth bowled Australia to their first win in England and the legend of the ashes was born.

The Australian tour of England in 1878 attracted little attention and when they lost by an innings to Nottinghamshire in their opening match, the result was as expected. Then, in a match at the end of May, they beat the MCC by nine wickets at Lords, having dismissed them for 33 and 19 runs in two innings. F. R. Spofforth took ten wickets for 20 runs in the match and was hailed in *Scores and Biographies* as 'one of the best, fastest and straightest bowlers that has ever entered the tented field'.

Spofforth, then 25 years old, was much more than a tear-away fast bowler. As a teenager he had copied the style of Tarrant who was on the England tour of Australia in 1863/64, and bowled as fast as he could until he was influenced by the medium and slow bowling of Alfred Shaw and Southerton. Combining elements of all three styles he became the most influential bowler of his generation and without his genius Australian cricket would not have come of age when it did.

In the Oval test match of 1882, that Australia won by seven runs, Spofforth took seven wickets in each innings for a total of 90 runs and inflicted the first defeat of England on home soil. The spoof notice that appeared in *The Times* announcing the death and cremation of English cricket caught the imagination and the mythical ashes were created.

On the 17 and 18 June 1878, the day before the match at Maldon, Spofforth had been playing for Australia at the Prince's ground in Chelsea against the Gentlemen of England, who included Hornby and Grace. Clearly, Thornton was very closely connected at this level of cricket, but it is not clear how the connection with Maldon had come about. From the late 1860s Maldon had looked increasingly towards the capital for its fixtures and it can only be assumed that some of the players not only became acquainted with Thornton, but sufficiently impressed him to bring such players to the town.

The remainder of the visiting eleven was drawn from the Orleans club at Twickenham, of which Thornton was patron, and where he provided games for his wide circle of cricketing colleagues. The ground was in the park that had previously been owned by the French royal family and it was opened to the public free of charge when Orleans played the Australians in July 1878. When Orleans played Rickling Green in 1882, it rattled up the record club score of 920 runs.

Powys, reckoned to be the fastest bowler in the land, had played with Thornton since university days but played little county cricket. Clarke and possibly Shepherd were Surrey players and Smith featured for Middlesex, while Posno and the Hungarian Foa brothers largely confined themselves to club cricket for Orleans.

Maldon had engaged John Hughes, who had helped them to victory over All England. Although almost 53 years of age, Hughes was still playing for Hertfordshire and was rated among the best of bowlers. He would continue for another 16 years until he played his final game for Hertford against his old club, Bishops Stortford, at the age of 69. The professional, Ted Pooley, highly rated as a wicketkeeper batsman for Surrey and the United South of England, was employed for the game and Henry Rowan, an Irishman who was a fringe player for Essex, also played for Maldon.

Pooley was a top class performer, but a difficult character who had a quick temper and language not always befitting the occasion. He went on tour to Australia under James Lillywhite in 1876/77, but instead of playing in the first official test match at Melbourne, he was detained in a New Zealand prison as a result of a betting scam and a violent bar-room brawl.[4] He escaped with a fine but had to travel home alone to England.

The match at Maldon was played on 19 June, the same day that Essex started a two day match against Suffolk at Brentwood. Silcock, Escott, Stevens and Roberts, all of whom had strong Maldon connections, were playing for the County and thus could not be brought in for the town. The team was, therefore, made up of regular Maldon players, Tomlinson, Handley, Reeve, Self, Sewell, Timperley and Henry and James Gower. Thomas Gower stood as umpire with Mr Ashley and the scorers were Mr Betts and Master Sadler.

In the preceding days, the weather had been wet but the pitch had been protected by tarpaulins and Thornton's men were pleasantly surprised to find that the Fairfield was so good a ground. Spofforth said it was the best pitch he had played on in England, but his tongue may have been firmly in his cheek as he proceeded to rip through Maldon's batting.

Tomlinson won the toss and chose to bat. At half past eleven, Spofforth bowled the first ball of the match to Handley, who scored a single off his third ball, giving strike to Alfred Self, who drove the last ball of the over for two. The overs were of five balls and Grace bowled a maiden to Handley before the demon got into his stride in the second over, dismissing Self and Pooley with consecutive deliveries.

Handley showed some good touches in his innings of 14 and Timperley and Gower each scored six, but the bowling was far too good and the innings crumbled to a total of 32

---

4. In the betting scam that he 'worked off against the unwary' before a match, Pooley would give odds of a pound to a shilling that he could predict the score of each home player. He would then give each player's score as nought and claim £1 for each duck (there were a lot of those!) and offer a 1/- (5p) for any other score made. In New Zealand the locals refused to be conned and a fight started when they wouldn't pay up. Pooley was a tragically flawed character who ended his days in the workhouse

13. John Hughes, Ted Pooley and Billy Oscroft. Three great professionals who appeared for Maldon in their prestige matches of the 1870s and 1880s.

runs. Spofforth had taken seven wickets for 17 runs and Grace three for 13; Thornton, unusually, kept wicket and allowed just one bye.

Thornton's Eleven, in their turn, found batting equally difficult, especially against Hughes' 'peculiar slows'. By the luncheon interval they were five wickets down for 50 runs, with Grace, Thornton, Spofforth and Hornby all dismissed. Hughes had taken four wickets, including two ebullient stumpings by Pooley, while Timperley had taken the important wicket of Thornton.

Over lunch at Mr Revett's, King's Head, Thornton spoke in complimentary terms of the Fairfield ground and the careful organization that had gone into the match. Tomlinson had previously thanked Thornton for bringing such famous players to Maldon, especially Spofforth, about whom he 'had heard so much in connection with the Australian team'. He apologised for the absence of players at the County match but professed that his team 'had done their best, though a very poor best he was afraid it was'.

After the interval, Clarke, Shepherd and Powys steered the eleven to a total of 100 runs, with Hughes taking six wickets for 35 runs off 23 overs. Maldon's second innings was opened by Self and Rowan, against the fast bowling of Powys and Hornby, who quickly removed the top order before 'the demon' was recalled to finish the job. Only Self, who made ten, and 14 runs scored for the last two wickets enabled the score to reach a miserable total of 38. Thornton's Eleven had won by an innings and 30 runs but, sportingly, they batted again to entertain the crowd with some attacking play by Grace, Thornton and Hornby, who had made 77 runs between them when play ended at six o'clock.

Although Maldon could not match the talents of the visitors, they were clearly impressed by the club and several of them returned to play in subsequent years. A game arranged for 1879 fell victim to the foul weather that swept the country that year but, in 1880, Thornton returned to Maldon with a team that included Powys, A. J. Webbe and G. F. Vernon of Middlesex and England, C. M. Kemp of Kent and one of the Walker brothers of Southgate. Maldon engaged Oscroft, the Nottinghamshire and All England Eleven batsman who had played at the Fairfield in 1873, Selby and Hughes, to strengthen their team, for which only Handley, Timperley, Self and James Gower remained from 1878. Oscroft hit a memorable 99 runs and Handley 26 out of a total of 198. Time ran out

14. No man could cut a ball late more cleverly. A. J. Webbe of Middlesex and England came with Thornton's Eleven to the Fairfield in 1881.

with the reply at 81 runs for four wickets, of which Vernon had made 38 and Thornton 24.

In July 1881, Thornton, Webbe, Vernon, Powys and the Foa brothers returned to Maldon with P. J. T. Henery, the Cambridge University blue who later played for Middlesex. The Maldon professionals were Potter of Surrey and Marten, who had first played for Colchester & Essex in the 1860s.

Maldon scored 144, with contributions from Beale (30) and Handley (26), but Orleans struck a rapid 224, dominated by 90 from Thornton and 48 from Henery in an opening partnership of 132. In the time remaining Maldon made a groggy 19 runs for four wickets.

The last match of the series was played on Thursday, 13 July 1882, when Thornton returned with Webbe, Vernon and Posno and newcomers, H. E. Rhodes of Kent and his cousin, Percy Thornton, who was secretary of the Middlesex club between 1870 and 1898.

Maldon again employed Marten, together with G. G. Hearne, the Kent professional who toured South Africa with the England team in 1891/92, and H. R. R. Bagot, an Essex player between 1880 and 1884.

Against bowling described as 'very weak', Hearne made 40 runs and Bagot (who arrived late) 25 not out of a Maldon total of 120. After lunch, Thornton was at his formidable best, twice hitting the ball over the rooftops and into the back gardens of houses in Fambridge Road, in an innings of 131. Orleans finished the day on 245 runs for eight wickets.

During the traditional lunch at the King's Head, Thornton read out a letter from 'the demon', F. R. Spofforth, who was again touring England with the Australians. He regretted not being able to play in the match at Maldon but sent his best wishes to the club, to which Thornton added the regards of E. M. Grace and the other cricketers who had played at the Fairfield over the years. Thornton and his Orleans men did not return to Maldon again.

Maldon versus C. I. Thornton's Eleven: played at the Fairfield, Maldon, on Wednesday, 19 June 1878

Maldon	*First innings*		
F. Handley		b. Spofforth	14
A. Self	lbw.	b. Spofforth	2
E. Pooley		b. Spofforth	0
C. R. Timperley	c. Spofforth	b. Grace	6
H. Gower	c. E. Foa	b. Grace	6
J. Hughes		b. Spofforth	0
H. B. Rowan	run out		0
W. Sewell	c. E. Foa	b. Spofforth	0
J. Gower		b. Spofforth	1
C. Reeve		b. Spofforth	0
T. Tomlinson	not out		1
Extras	b.1, l.b.1		2
	Total		**32**

Bowling analysis: five ball overs

	Overs	*Maidens*	*Runs*	*Wickets*
F. R. Spofforth	13	2 or 3	17	7
E. M. Grace	12	4	13	2

Thornton's XI			
E. M. Grace		b. Hughes	7
B. Posno	c. & b.	Hughes	13
C. I. Thornton	c. Hughes	b. Timperley	13
F. R. Spofforth	st. Pooley	b. Hughes	9
A. N. Hornby	st. Pooley	b. Hughes	0
M. C. Clarke	not out		23
F. Shepherd	run out		11
W. N. Powys		b. Self	16
E. Foa		b. Hughes	3
G. Foa	c. Sewell	b. Hughes	0
C. Smith		b. Self	1
Extras	b.3, l.b.1		4
	Total		**100**

	Overs	*Maidens*	*Runs*	*Wickets*
J. Hughes	23	9	35	6
C. R. Timperley	18	0	51	1
A. Self	4.1	1	10	2

Maldon	*Second innings*		
A. Self	c. Thornton	b. Hornby	10
H. B. Rowan	c. Thornton	b. Hornby	3
C. R. Timperley		b. Powys	0
F. Handley		b. Spofforth	0
E. Pooley		b. Hornby	0
H. Gower	c. Smith	b. Hornby	5
J. Gower		b. Spofforth	2
W. Sewell	c. Spofforth	b. Hornby	1
C. Reeve		b. Spofforth	6
J. Hughes	not out		4
T. Tomlinson		b. Spofforth	4
Extras	b.3		3
	Total		**38**

	Overs	*Maidens*	*Runs*	*Wickets*
W. N. Powys	3	0	8	1
A. N. Hornby	10	1	12	5
F. R. Spofforth	7.3	0	15	4

C. I. Thornton's Eleven won by an innings and 30 runs.

(In an exhibition second innings in the time remaining, Grace made 7, Spofforth 27 and Hornby 43, against the assorted bowling of Self, Reeve, Tomlinson, Hughes and Timperley.)

Chapter 19

Frank Silcock's benefit 1878

For three days in September 1878, some of the giants of Victorian cricket gathered at Witham to pay homage to Frank Silcock, Maldon's professional between 1861 and 1867. In recognition of his services to the game, a benefit match was organized under the patronage of the MCC, whose members inaugurated his benefit fund with a donation of £20. Such was Silcock's standing that his other patrons included Lord Braybrook of Audley End, James Round, Charles Du Cane and the Hon. E. H. Grimston. The *Chelmsford Chronicle* described him thus:

> There is no professional cricketer living who has combined such popularity with gentlemanly bearing in the cricketing world, as Silcock, and no one is more entitled to a benefit than he.

Silcock had risen to become a regular member of the United South of England Eleven, a team dominated in the 1870s by the Grace brothers, notably by W. G., who agreed to bring the Eleven to play Eighteen Gentlemen of Essex in the benefit match. He kept his promise to bring a strong side, as follows:

W. G. Grace (captain, age 30 – Gloucestershire and England)
G. F. Grace (age 28 – Gloucestershire and England)
W. R. Gilbert (age 25 – Gloucestershire and Australian tour)
F. W. Bush (age 26 – Surrey and two West Indian tours)
H. Charlwood (age 32 – 'Hope of Sussex' and England)
G. Elliott (age 28 – Kent and Surrey)
R. Humphrey (age 30 – Surrey and Australian tour)

H. Jupp (age 37 – Surrey and England)
W. G. Marten (age 33 – Kent, Surrey and Essex)
E. Pooley (age 40 –Surrey and American and Australian tours)
J. Southerton (Surrey, Sussex, Hampshire and England).

G. F. Grace was the youngest of the brothers, a brilliant player who made his first-class debut at the age of 15 and played for England in 1880. Tragically, he died from a congested lung later that year, on his way to play at Winchester. W. R. Gilbert was a cousin to the Graces and accompanied W. G. on the Australian tour of 1873/74.

Assembling the Essex team was more problematic. As the newspaper reported, 'September is not a good month for cricket ... as gentlemen throw aside the ball and willow for the dog and gun', and 40 invitations were sent out before an Eighteen could be enticed from field and moor. C. R. Stevens, who had appeared variously for Colchester and Maldon and was secretary of the Witham club in 1878, was Silcock's main support in organizing the game. They employed the evergreen John Hughes from Bishops Stortford and 17-year-old Thomas Burgess, a professional at Harrogate, who went on to play for Yorkshire in 1895.

Of the Gentlemen's team that reported to the ground on the day, eleven players represented Essex in 1878/79. They were:

James Round (captain)
K. Borrowes
G. H. Candler
F. Capel-Cure
D. C. Davey
J. Dixon
T. Earps
C. H. S. Escott (the former Maldon player)
W. Howard

C. G. Merewether
C. R. Stevens

The team was completed by Lord Hamilton, Reverend J. W. B. Laurie and Messrs. Collin, Fort, Hardy, Hutley and Shee, so that the Eighteen had grown to a team of twenty!

Witham had been chosen as a location central to the clubs where Silcock had played in his early years. The park of Witham House was reckoned to have as good a cricket wicket as anywhere in the County and was only a short walk from the mainline railway station to London. Ground preparation had been in the hands of the Head Park Keeper, Charlie Roberts (a capable cricketer himself) and, interestingly, a boundary rope was used to define the playing area, even though boundaries were not officially introduced into the laws until 1884.

The first morning, Thursday, 12 September, was greeted with leaden skies and driving rain but play was possible at 1.15 p.m. when Round won the toss, and the band of the 11th Hussars gave way to Escott and Stevens, opening the batting for the 'Twenty'. Two interruptions by rain driven by gale force winds preceded the lunch interval, taken at 3.15 p.m., with the telegraph at 20 runs without loss of wickets.

In the afternoon, Stevens completed a fine 53, but only Round (12) and Burgess (21) reached double figures, as the Essex Gentlemen finished the day on a total of 142 runs for 15 wickets. The following morning, in fine weather, they reached a total of 175, thanks to 15 runs from Candler and 12 not out from Hughes. W. G. had bowled 60 four ball overs and taken 15 wickets for 71 runs; the other wicket takers were Gilbert, G. F. Grace and Southerton, whose 43 overs had cost just 36 runs.

At two minutes past one, W. G. and his cousin, W. R. Gilbert, opened the innings for the Eleven against the bowling of Hughes and Stevens, who soon bowled Gilbert for three runs. W. G. followed soon afterwards, run out for ten, having misjudged the fielding of his hit to leg. Further wickets fell to leave the Eleven reeling at 57 runs for five wickets, when Humphrey (32) and Charlwood (43) came together to repair the innings. The lower order offered no resistance and the innings closed at 5.15 p.m. for a total of 134 runs, a first innings deficit of 41. John Hughes had bowled 50 overs throughout the afternoon, taking three wickets for 63 runs, the other wickets being shared between Stevens, Burgess and Earps.

Hughes and Candler opened the Twenty's second innings, but Hughes was caught at long on by Charlwood off W.G. before the close, when the total was 21 runs. When play was resumed in fine weather on the Saturday, runs flowed from the bats of the Gentlemen, with Borrowes making 88 runs and Capel-Cure and Lord Hamilton each scoring 33 out of a total of 235 runs. W. G. had taken a further 11 wickets for 127 runs off 51 overs, with Southerton and Bush each taking four wickets.

There being no provision in the laws for declarations, the United South of England Eleven was left with the impossible task of scoring 277 runs to win in the two remaining hours of the match. W. G. showed willing, driving Hughes' first ball for four, but when he tried to repeat the stroke off the next ball, he was caught in the deep by Burgess. George Grace came in and played some strokes until he too was caught off Hughes, by Round at mid-on. Bush hit 26, but when Humphrey and Charlwood went cheaply, Pooley and Southerton went onto the defensive to play out time, when the score was 65 runs for five wickets. The match was drawn 'in favour of the Gentlemen'.

Despite the appalling weather on the first day, more than 3000 people came to watch the play. They had seen the legendary W. G. Grace living out his reputation as a cricketer greedy for success in cricket at all levels. Having failed with the bat he proceeded to bowl 111 overs in the match and add 26 wickets to his personal tally. There was no generosity expected or given in this sort of match and Round, having the services of Hertfordshire's John Hughes available to him, bowled him for 76 overs. Hughes, at 53 years of age, proved yet again that he was among the best bowlers in the land, teasing and dismissing some of the finest batsmen of the Victorian era.

The benefit marked the end of Frank Silcock's career with the United South of England Eleven but he continued to command a place in the Essex team. Even at the age of 46, when Essex moved their headquarters from Brentwood to Leyton, he was engaged to play and gave such service to the club that he was granted a second benefit match in 1893.

Part 4

Into the Twentieth Century

Chapter 20

Professionals in club cricket

Since the earliest days, strong feelings have been aroused by the use of paid players in recreational cricket. During the mid-Victorian period the top clubs routinely engaged professionals even though they were frowned upon in earlier times. By the twentieth century Maldon was no longer among the top clubs and gave no thought to players of that class, even though Maldon Strollers encountered Hey, a Nottinghamshire professional, playing for the army at Colchester Garrison in 1949.

The strong clubs had employed professionals earlier in the twentieth century. At the start of the 1924 season, the three big Braintree clubs, Courtaulds, Crittalls and Braintree Town had completed their signings, although some controversy surrounded Ted Eaton, who had previously played as a professional for Witham. The Town club claimed he had joined them as an amateur so as not to transgress the custom of limiting the number of paid players.

After the First World War, powerful works clubs, funded by industrial money, were among the best. As well as Courtaulds and Crittalls at Braintree, Hoffmans, Marconi and Cromptons provided high class cricket facilities for their employees at Chelmsford. Although Maldon had the facilities of its major employers, Bentalls and Sadds, the ambitions of these firms did not extend beyond departmental and village cricket for their workers.

The first professionals emerged in the early 1700s when the nobility adopted the game from their servants. Aristocratic patrons scoured the countryside to buy up the best cricketing talent to work on their estates, nominally as grooms, gamekeepers or bailiffs, though their main purpose was to win cricket matches for their employer. With normal prize money of 500 guineas (£100,000 today) and enormous scope for all manner of side-bets, cricket was a serious business for the early patrons.

Maldon played for rather less prize money. Fifty guineas was the stake for the series of matches against Purleigh in the 1780s and 1790s, enough money to pay the wages of a building craftsman for seven years! There is no evidence that paid players were brought in to win these matches but who knows what inducements were given to 'Mr Tabrum of Shopland' to bring him from Southend to represent Maldon in 1789?

Similarly, as Purleigh was allowed to pick players from Latchingdon, Stow, Danbury, Woodham Mortimer, Rettendon and Stock, who knows what deals were cut in the smoky back rooms of country inns? The match of 1789 was unfinished so it was necessary to arrange another game at Purleigh in September. When Maldon made only 38 runs against Purleigh's 112, the odds against them rose to 10 to 1. Confounding the odds, Maldon dismissed Purleigh for 41 in the second innings and knocked off the runs to win. What drunken celebrations there would have been among the winners in the Purleigh Bell that night.

Gambling fever gripped all levels of Georgian society and some precautions had to be taken against cheating. In order to keep out paid ringers, cricket challenges usually stipulated that 'only men of the town' could represent their clubs in money matches. In challenging Ingatestone in 1789, Maldon was careful to insist that only 'eleven who have been resident six months in Ingatestone' could participate in a match. Ingatestone apparently had the reputation of lodging men in the town for the summer in their drive for prize money.

As sure as night followed day, corruption scandals followed the craze for high stakes and frenzied gambling. By the beginning of the nineteenth century, when war clouds gathered over the English Channel and troop movements rather than cricket occupied the minds of the people of Maldon, professional cricketers entered their own darkest hour. Young professionals, brought by their masters from Sussex and Hampshire to play in the great matches at Lords, were bought by bookmakers in the taverns where they stayed. Individual performances were doctored, matches were sold and the integrity of cricket sunk to its lowest ebb.

In the resultant clean up, bookmakers were banned from Lords and a veil of Victorian respectability was drawn over the episode. Local reaction was also predictable. Cricket was reasserted as a game for the enjoyment of gentlemen who would play among themselves for the 'love and honour of the game'. Thus in 1852, when Maldon was drawing up its list of opponents for the summer, it invited clubs within 16 miles of the town to make a match, but stressed 'no professional players to be allowed on either side'.

By 1861, the thinking had changed. Frank Silcock was engaged as Maldon's professional and the club's rise to prominence began in earnest. Silcock was one of several professionals on the club circuit in the 1860s. Foster appeared for Colchester in 1862 and 1863, to be replaced by William Marten who represented Kent and Surrey before returning to Essex in 1876. Marten played for many clubs and representative teams and was a 'given' professional for the Gentlemen of Essex in Frank Silcock's benefit match in 1878.

As club games were infrequent by today's standards and cricket was played every day of the week (except Sundays) professionals moved from club to club to earn a living. Marten played against Maldon for Witham, who also engaged Goodhew and Isted, both of whom could be found in the Maldon ranks when a little extra strength was needed. Professionals might also be 'given' to the opposition to even the odds, as in the match against Springfield in 1863 when Maldon, strengthened by several Colchester players, gave Frank Silcock to the opposition because their main bowler was ill.

In the event, Silcock took only the wickets of Alfred Self and Captain Probert, but he gave 'the Maldon gentlemen a tremendous amount of leather hunting' in a hard hit innings of 62 runs. Springfield won the game by 121 runs.

After Silcock's departure from the Fairfield, the Maldon club did not engage another professional on a permanent basis. Generally their home-grown talent was sufficient to match other clubs, although the likes of Goodhew or Isted were used when the situation demanded. Tomlinson also called upon the Irishman, O'Leary, to even the odds of a game against Mr Page's Eleven at Down Hall. Professionals were generally engaged to bowl in the better country house matches and, when Maldon travelled to Thorndon Hall in 1870, there were no less than three: Frank Silcock, his cousin Joe and John Bristow, the Surrey man, playing for the opposition.

For the great matches of the 1870s, Maldon engaged some of the leading professionals of the time. Against the All England Eleven in 1873, Frank Silcock, then playing with the United South of England Eleven, returned with his old mentor, John Hughes, to rout the travelling professionals. Against 'Buns' Thornton's Eleven in 1878, John Hughes could not recapture the same success, despite having the services of the volatile Surrey stumper, Ted Pooley to assist him.

Against Thornton's Orleans team the following year John Hughes appeared again, this time in company with Billy Oscroft, the Nottinghamshire professional who had visited the Fairfield with the All England Eleven and one Selby, possibly another Nottinghamshire professional who played six times for England between 1876 and 1882. For the match in 1881, Maldon was strengthened by Joseph Potter of Surrey and the familiar face of William Marten. Marten returned in 1882 for the final match against Thornton's team with George Hearne, who scored nearly 10,000 runs and took nearly 700 wickets for Kent between 1875 and 1895. Hearne played once for England in South Africa in 1891/92.

The years of the Thornton matches seemed to mark the beginning of the decline of the Maldon club. Tomlinson, while still nominally captain of the team, appeared less and less

15. Cricket's bleak mid-winter. Impromptu cricket games between Maldon and Heybridge were sometimes played on the ice at the Fullbridge during hard winters at the end of the nineteenth century.

frequently on the field. Other fine players like Henry Gower and Alfred Self were reaching the end of their playing days and handing over to a new generation that could not quite match their talents. For 100 years the question of professionals in the game did not concern the Maldon clubs that emerged in the twentieth century.

It was not until the new Maldon cricket club entered the top echelon of the Two Counties Championship in 1988 that professionals were again encountered and the club themselves began to import fringe players from Essex County Cricket Club and from the Australian Grade club, Waverley, in Sydney.

Chapter 21
The cricket family Gower

There is one name that reappears in the records of Maldon cricket across the centuries, and that name is Gower. A Mr Gowers played for Maldon against Dengie Hundred back in 1790 and he played against Purleigh in 1796 for a match stake of 50 guineas. Worth around £10,000 today, the stake was typical for contests between local clubs at the turn of the eighteenth century. In the twentieth century, Tony Gower played for both Maldon Town and Old Maldonians cricket clubs, before becoming a vice-president of the new Maldon cricket club that was formed in 1976.

It is not known whether the Mr Gowers who played in the 1790s was the founding father of the cricketing dynasty but the line can be traced with certainty back to Tony's great grandfather, John, who was born in 1806. John had five sons, Henry, William, John, James and Thomas, all of whom played some cricket for Maldon during the Victorian era when the club was at its most powerful. William first played in 1862, John in 1865, and James a few years later. Thomas' only recorded match was in 1866, but he had the distinction of standing as umpire for the famous players in the match against C. I. Thornton's XI in 1878.

The most talented of the brothers was Henry, who was born in 1840 and made his debut in the country house match at Woodham Mortimer Place in 1859. In 1860, he made 14 and 23 against Purleigh, significant scores in habitually low scoring games, but at Billericay he made only two before being dismissed by journeyman professional, Frank Silcock. The following year Silcock was engaged as Maldon's professional and his coaching was to be of lasting benefit to Henry Gower and other young players at Maldon. Later in his career Silcock proved his coaching ability with appointments at Felsted, Uppingham and Eton schools.

In 1866 Henry played with brother John against the recently formed Essex county club at Colchester. Maldon won the match by 24 runs, thanks mainly to Frank Silcock's eight wickets, although the Gower brothers contributed 20 of Maldon's 99 runs against professional bowling. Henry continued to represent Maldon in most of their matches for another 20 years, sometimes in the same side as one or other of his brothers. In 1868, his growing reputation earned him an invitation to play for Twenty-two of Chelmsford against the All-England Eleven.

Alfred Self of Maldon was also invited to play in the match for which Chelmsford had been 'given' two professionals, William McIntyre of Nottinghamshire and William Slinn of Yorkshire, a bowling legend who had once taken all ten wickets for Harrogate against All-England. Frank Silcock's cousin Joe was also in the Chelmsford Twenty-two, together with cricket luminaries such as Lord Petre of Ingatestone and James Round.

Lillywhite's *Scores and Biographies* comments, 'This was the worst wicket with one exception, the All England Eleven had to play on this season.' It was no surprise, therefore, that Slinn and McIntyre bundled out the Eleven for 28 runs in their first innings, after Henry Gower had been one of only three men to reach double figures in the Chelmsford total of 92 runs. In the second innings he made three out of a total of 75 runs that left All England needing 140 to win in their second innings. Slinn took another six wickets to give him 12 in the match and McIntyre took three as they dismissed the Eleven for 101, giving Chelmsford victory by 38 runs.

Henry played again, this time for Eighteen of Maldon, against the All England Eleven in 1873 but was bowled for just one and four by Nottinghamshire's Fred Morley, who took 21 wickets in the match. Maldon won the match by 132 runs though, thanks to their two professionals, Frank Silcock and John Hughes, whose fine bowling exploited showery conditions.

Five years later Henry was joined by brother John in the second great Maldon match, against C. I. Thornton's Eleven. John was twice bowled for a duck by Australian legend, Fred Spofforth, while Henry managed six and five. He did manage to keep out Spofforth, but fell to catches off the bowling of E. M. Grace in the first innings and of A. N. Hornby in the second. Third brother, Thomas, probably chose the best option by umpiring the match that Thornton's XI won by an innings and 30 runs.

As the nineteenth century drew to a close and Henry Gower and his contemporaries retired, Maldon's reputation on the cricket field began to diminish. Some of the new generation of Gowers continued to play but reports of matches began to peter out. By the time the new Grammar School was built on the northern part of the Fairfield in 1907, the club had deep problems of finance and playing strength.

Happily, a revival occurred in 1923 when Maldon Town Cricket Club was relaunched. By then, Tony Gower's father, Stanley (son of Henry), had moved to Norfolk but his cousin, Jack, became the rising star of Maldon cricket. His heavy scoring on the local circuit between the wars earned Jack an Essex trial but, as a professional accountant, he opted for job security and tormenting opposition bowlers.

When Tony returned to Maldon the Town club was playing on the Promenade on the site where the bowling green and tennis courts were subsequently built. As a stroke-making opening batsman he became an integral part of the strong Town club that emerged after the Second World War. The pitch was to his liking in those days because the Borough Engineer was in the team and kept the park keeper on his toes!

Unfortunately the support of the Council was short-lived and the club was condemned to wandering status when the bowling green was laid. After several years without a home a sharing arrangement with Maldon Town Social & Athletic

16. Heybridge Cricket Club in 1907. By the early 1900s, Heybridge had become the progressive club in the town. Standing: (left to right) F. Mott (scorer), A. Gymer, E. Linnett, F. Chalk, C. Fenn, W. Gill (umpire). Sitting: T. Gill, E. B. Cheales, Rev. A. P. McNeile, F. C. Perry (captain), A. Ward, C. Algar and W. Livermore.

Club on the Wallace Binder Playing Field off Fambridge Road was agreed. Tony became captain of the club at about this time but regrettably the spirit of earlier years was lacking. There were still some good players at the club but the effect of Sunday cricket that had been introduced after the war was to weaken the Saturday team. Another frustration was that young players were all called away for national military service so that it was difficult to field a settled team.

In 1958, after an unhappy few years at Fambridge Road, the Maldon Town cricket club was disbanded and Tony with several of his playing colleagues joined the Old Maldonians club that had been formed for ex-pupils of the grammar school. Matches were played on the school playing field (the old Fairfield) for several seasons before arrangements were made to share the Promenade ground with Maldon Strollers Cricket Club.

Tony Gower captained the Old Maldonians in the 1960s and thus takes some credit for the younger generation of cricketers whose initiative lay behind the formation of the new Maldon cricket club. Unfortunately the local Gower line ends with Tony and there are no young Gowers to carry the family cricket tradition into the twenty-first century.

Chapter 22

The summers of 1902 and 1903

In the year that Edward VII became King and Victor Trumper illuminated the wet English summer with the genius of his strokeplay, Maldon – the town and the cricket club – were facing intractable problems. From the carefree days when cricket was in its infancy, the town's economic significance had eroded away. In 1797, the Chelmer canal had bypassed Maldon and, 50 years later, the new railway created a fast and flexible system of inland transport.

By the 1850s, trade through the port had returned to the levels of the pre-boom years and Maldon had again assumed the character of a market town. Then in 1874, agriculture, which had experienced a temporary revival in its economic fortunes, was dealt a hammer blow when price controls on corn were abandoned and the livelihoods of local farmers and landowners were threatened by cheap American imports. A second blow occurred in 1880 when port status was taken away from Maldon. Although perhaps not significant in practical terms, the effect on Maldon's standing was humiliating when it was designated a mere creek serving the port of Colchester.

The following year financial scandal hit the town when the South Essex Investment & Advance Company was wound up, losing Maldon's honest citizens some £90,000 (perhaps £6m today) of their savings. The Company was a building society managed by some of the same men with interests in legal, financial and the affairs of the town corporation. Not surprisingly the mood of the town in the 1880s became 'surly and irritable' and 'to some Maldonians the Council was simply the public face of that nebulous group known as "the forty thieves"'.

The Council was rife with mean minded and jealous infighting and showed little capacity to tackle its own problems of financial irregularity and debt incurred in schemes for sewerage and highway improvement, enforced upon it by Government inspectors.

Why should all this matter to the cricket club? The ruling body of the Victorian club had always comprised some of the worthies that served on the council. The initiative for the All England Eleven match came from twice Mayor, Humpherys, with the backing of several fellow councillors. By the 1870s, Tomlinson and Self – to name but two of the regular players – had been elected to the council and the cricket club was part of the Maldon establishment.

Tomlinson retained control of the cricket club until he was 60 years of age, despite his less frequent appearances on the field and his growing involvement in the corporation's affairs. By 1875 he had become the town's Surgeon and Medical Officer, Public Vaccinator for the St Mary's District and Surgeon to the Workhouse. A growing agenda of civic commitments and an air of depression around the town could hardly have refreshed the energy and ambition for cricket that he had shown 30 years before.

By the time Tomlinson finally stood down as captain of cricket in 1890, all the players who had achieved the rise to prominence had died or retired and the strength of the club waned. Alfred Self, after some abrasive business and civic dealings, committed suicide in 1901 after the death of his wife. Only the Gower name achieved some continuity into the twentieth century as the Maldon club struggled along from season to season, retaining some good opponents but rarely performing well against them.

By 1902 Maldon had changed irrevocably. The firms of E. H. Bentall and John Sadd & Sons had grown in international importance to become the major employers of the town's inhabitants and the touchstone of the local economy. The corporation had sunk its aspirations into the Promenade (opened in 1895) and had succeeded in attracting tourists to the town via the new railway line into the Dengie Hundred.

The population had trebled since the early 1700s and created an insatiable demand for cricket as clubs sprang up in works, villages, churches, schools and colleges. In the new working-class environment, Saturday cricket became the norm and organized leagues were formed in various parts of Essex, including Harlow, Tilbury and Colchester, where Frinton, Wivenhoe, West Mersea and Great Bentley were among the participants. The Maldon club showed little interest in the changes in the world around it and stuck doggedly to traditional ways.

By 1902 the club was truly in the doldrums. There were insufficient members to field a regular eleven and funds depended upon a production of the operetta, *Daisy Dell* that raised £16. Subscriptions were increased to ten shillings (50p) at the Annual Meeting in May when Mr F. H. Bright, then the serving Town Clerk, became president and Mr Hawkes and Mr Eve agreed to share the administrative duties. Mr Harvey Crabbe, the leading batsman from 1901 with 349 runs from 12 innings, was elected captain and Mr W. Blaxall, his deputy. Presentations were made to Crabbe and to the leading bowler, H. Eve, who had taken 27 wickets at an average of 12 runs apiece the previous season. Other players mentioned in match reports for 1902 were Gower, Keen, Pyman, Richardson, Ward, Boreham, Woodcraft, Cocks, Cheales and Samms.

Two matches are worthy of note. Against Colchester in May, Maldon replied to a total of 201 runs for six wickets with 30 for two when rain intervened. In July Maldon lost by 60 runs after dismissing Colchester for 158 runs.

The local derby between Maldon and Heybridge was played out over three matches. Heybridge had won one and one had been drawn when the final game was staged in August. Maldon made 153 runs for nine wickets, thanks to contributions from

17. Cattle on the hallowed turf. Loving care had been replaced by more rudimentary methods at the Fairfield by the end of the eighteenth century.

Pyman, Eve, Crabbe and Richardson, the wickets being shared between Cocks and Chalk. In their turn Heybridge had made 118 for four with Ward, Boreham and Woodcraft all scoring well when time elapsed and the match was drawn.

In 1903, Maldon thrashed Heybridge twice, bowling them out for totals of just 23 and 29 runs in two low scoring matches. Nevertheless, when the Colchester club came forward with the idea of an East Anglian League that season, it was to Heybridge, rather than Maldon, that it issued an invitation.

The Colchester town club was clearly dissatisfied with the quality of cricket played in their local league and continued to arrange their own games against the bigger clubs in the County. Ipswich, Chelmsford and Harwich supported the formation of the new elite league but Maldon, who had been among Colchester's opposition the previous year, were clearly seen as lacking the potential for that level of competition. Heybridge on the other hand seem to have gained the reputation of a go-ahead club of some ability who were committed to the new reality of competitive Saturday cricket.

The plans for the new elite league did not materialise so that cricket at Maldon and Heybridge carried on much as before. Proof of Maldon's decline from glory came in a festival week fixture at Witham, where the old enemy ran up a total of 182 runs for eight wickets. In response the men of Maldon were bowled out for 20 runs.

Chapter 23

Slipping into obscurity

Although Maldon experienced some relief from the economic depression that had gripped the town for two decades, the cricket club failed to reflect this regeneration when the Edwardian era dawned. The club hung on to some good quality fixtures with the likes of Colchester, Chelmsford and Witham but were too weak to do them justice.

Membership had dwindled and money was a constant problem. Season to season existence depended upon fund raising events like bazaars, dances and even an operetta. The club muddled along on memories of the past while the world changed rapidly around it. Neighbouring village clubs began to thrive on Saturday cricket but the Maldon club, comprising mostly local traders, clung to mid-week matches and ignored the vastly increased working class population of the town.

On the face of it, 1905 appeared to be a promising season. One hundred people attended the dance held at the end of April to raise funds and a list of 16 fixtures had been arranged. Home and away games had been agreed with Brentwood, Colchester, Danbury, Heybridge, Southminster, Terling, Wickford and Witham. A match with Chelmsford was also played during the season. The leading players were all-rounder, Hollister, batsmen, Blaxall, Cheales and Richardson, and bowlers, Mumford, Ward and J. H. Gower. Over the season, four matches were won, four drawn and seven lost, but there were some humiliations against the bigger clubs.

Chelmsford piled up a total of 205 runs for eight wickets and shot Maldon out for 23. It was not quite so bad against Witham, where Maldon managed to reach a total of 110 runs in response to Witham's 214.

Behind the scenes, however, money worries and conservative attitudes were wearing the club down. The annual subscription of ten shillings was well beyond the reach of working people and to maintain the exclusive nature of membership, the annual meeting of 1905 decided the subscriptions policy should be 'strictly enforced'. It cost about £40 a year to run the club and it was a serious blow when the fund raising dance of 1906 only attracted half the number who had attended the previous year.

The 1906 season carried on nevertheless with a good list of fixtures, but only one match report found its way into the local newspaper. That was a surprise win against Essex Club & Ground played on a July Wednesday when Maldon batted first and made 115 runs before dismissing the opposition for 60. Blaxall, Boreham, Gadsden and Harvey Crabbe all made a few runs but the victory belonged to Ward, who took eight wickets for 34 runs in the Club & Ground innings. Over the season, the Maldon club won nine out of 15 matches played.

Financially, there was a loss of £3 on the season and the honorary treasurer, Mr Saltmarsh, resigned his position at the annual meeting, as did Mr Anstey, the honorary secretary. No successors could be found and club president, Mr F. H. Bright, found himself in charge of a rudderless ship. He decided it was time to test the depth of the members' apathy with some crisis management and called an extraordinary general meeting in April 1907 'to consider whether the club should be allowed to drop'.

The theory of crisis management worked unswervingly as the members stepped back from the brink and, energised by their new *esprit de corps*, they resolved 'to carry on as before'. Mr Henry Wade stepped forward for the honorary secretary's position and Mr F. H. Hills filled the vacant post of honorary treasurer. It was in lighter and more confident mood that the members filed from the worries of the Blue Boar meeting room into the bar for the smoking concert that had been arranged for their enjoyment.

During the 1907 season, Maldon lost to Witham Second XI by 164 runs and were beaten twice by Great Baddow in low scoring games. Harvey Crabbe made 100 at Southminster where the club had a resounding victory, but the highlight of the season was a match against the Officers of the Fourth Essex Regiment. The gentlemen of Maldon could still command some social influence and civic leaders and men of business joined the twice bankrupt local dignitary and ageing adventurer, Sir Claude Champion de Crespigny in the marquee for tea.

More than 400 spectators also came to the Fairfield to watch the play and the marching of the regimental band. It is to be hoped that the band was in better form than the officers, who managed a total of 74 runs and 29 for four wickets in reply to Maldon's massive score of 193 runs for six wickets. A collection for club funds among the guests and spectators was doubtless thankfully received.

In September 1907 the Grammar School relocated from London Road to the new site on the Fairfield, where the present Upper Plume School stands. Assumptions that the cricket club were displaced by the new school are probably unfounded. There is no reference to any change of arrangements in the annual meeting reports that detailed the financial and organizational difficulties facing the club, and the school would not have needed so large an adjoining acreage for its relatively small pupil numbers.

Over the following few seasons, however, news of Maldon Cricket Club becomes very sketchy, although some very brief match reports appear in 1909 and 1910. Meanwhile, the Grammar School, that had initially struggled to attract sufficient pupil numbers and was threatened with closure, began to grow strong and cricket became an important tradition.

The *Maldon Advertiser* in 1913 carried reports of Maldon Grammar School matches against St Peter's Institute and against Maldon Tradesmen, but news of the Maldon club had disappeared from its pages. Perhaps the club continued to play low key matches until the Great War, but failed to form again until the early 1920s. In 1924, the Maldon Town cricket club resumed play for another 30 years before its problems again became too great to carry on.

Part 5

Voices of the Past

Chapter 24

Maldon Strollers Cricket Club

The early history of the Strollers club has been compiled with the help of recollections by three former players, Dennis Fenn, Tom Gozzett and Laurie Hardy-King.

Mr Fenn, by his own admission, 'never a great cricketer', was an important figure as honorary secretary of the club when his regular match reports gave a good account of events on the field. At the end of the 1949 season, the Sports Editor of the *Essex Chronicle* lamented,

> Cricket is over for the season. A pity, because I shall miss my contacts with two of the youngest and most capable Club Secretaries in these parts: Dennis Fenn and Frank Eaton [of Maldon Town].

Dennis later served for many years as secretary of the highly successful Heybridge Swifts Football Club.

Mr Gozzett, as well as having a sharp memory for cricket in the 1930s, also provides some interesting background on other sports in Maldon at the time. A huge athletics track lay behind Spital Road on the land subsequently taken for housing, where whippet racing was staged on Saturday evenings. The bowling green was situated off London Road and cricket was played on the Promenade and on the works grounds of Sadds, off the Causeway, and Bentalls behind the 'Wave' public house at Heybridge (now the Bentall Centre). As well as the main football clubs, Maldon and Heybridge Swifts, pitches were laid out at Champion Lodge, the home of the octogenarian adventurer, Sir Claude Champion de Crespigny, off Broad Street Green at Great Totham. Maldon Wesleyans played their soccer on this ground.

Maldon Wesleyans became the springboard for the formation of the Strollers club and Sir Claude, who had witnessed the last great days of the Maldon club of the 1880s, became its first president. The Wesleyan movement went back more than 200 years to the religious breakaway from the Church of England inspired by the evangelical preacher, John Wesley. In 1932, various factions of this movement came together to form the Methodist Church, uniting the separate churches that then existed at Maldon.

Tom Gozzett recalls 1932 also as being the year when the first steps towards the formation of Maldon Strollers were taken. Living as a boy at number 36 The Causeway, the garden of his house was the meeting point for the first discussion of a breakaway from the Wesleyan cricket club that had grown to occupy the boys of the church. As well as a distinctive religious structure, the Methodists had strong moral objections to alcohol and gambling and frowned on the sweepstakes and similar fund-raising schemes that were commonly used to support the running costs of sports clubs.

The men involved in those first discussions were George Gymer, Eddy Lewis and Frank Davis, although it was Bill Weavers who later claimed much of the credit for the growth of the early Strollers club. Be that as it may, it was Tom Gozzett, when he left school in 1934, who took on the task of selling sixpenny football cards to raise money for club funds. It was a time when he and his contemporaries looked with amazement at the growing range of cricket equipment in Pope & Smiths sports shop in Chelmsford and learned that cricket bats came in different qualities with both long and short handles!

The aptly named Strollers were a wandering club in the early days until steps were taken to lay a second square at the Promenade, adjoining the area used by the Maldon Town club.

18. Maldon Strollers in 1936. Standing: (left to right) Herbert Green, Alan Clarke, Bill Weavers, Joe Gozzett. Len Hipsey, Mr Taber (umpire), Hector Constantine. Sitting: Doug Gooch, Laurie Davies, George Gymer (captain), Eddie Lewis, Laurie Hardy-King, Dennis Fenn is sitting on the grass.

The turf for the new square according to popular recollection was cut from the nearby seawall, which may explain some of the problems that were experienced in later years.

Mr Hardy-King first played for the club as an enthusiastic 18-year-old in 1935, the first season of home matches on the Promenade. He became one of the Strollers most loyal and long-serving members and took over the captaincy of the team in 1950. Three years later he married and moved to Tollesbury where he still happily tends his lovely garden. In his youth – so keen was he to play cricket – he would turn out for Totham or Wickham Bishops when Strollers had no game and, on one occasion, he cycled to Totham for a morning match, home for lunch, and to Cold Norton for another match in the afternoon. On that day he might have been grateful for his father's horse and cart that could reputedly find its own way home from the many hostelries at away grounds!

Generally, however, cars were available for travel to away matches, although sometimes these had to be hired from Mr Stroud of Wickham Bishops, complete with lady chauffeur. Tom Gozzett, as a young teenager had the privilege of riding beside the lady driver, a position he had to give up to an even younger Dennis Fenn when he started playing! For more distant games a coach might be hired.

George Gymer was the captain of the team in 1935 and led them to 16 victories out of 24 matches played despite a very wet summer. Matches were often played out in rain that made pitches even more difficult than they normally were. Many games were won on a total of 50 runs and team totals in excess of 100 were only achieved in exceptionally good conditions. Even so the record of Tom's elder brother Joe's performances that season was remarkable: he took 108 wickets at an average of 4.94 runs apiece. Laurie Hardy-King, the leading batsman averaged just 11.86 runs an innings, closely followed by Frank Davis and Hector Constantine.

Good wins were recorded over established local club sides Tillingham and Hatfield Peverel, whose batsmen withered against the hostility of Joe Gozzett. Tillingham tumbled for just 47 runs (Gozzett 5 for 19) and Hatfield Peverel totalled a humiliating 24 (Gozzett 6 for 7). Elsewhere, there was a remarkable game at Margaretting where Hardy-King scored 30 not out from a total of 37 made in response to the home side's 103 runs. After a long journey to Brentwood Gas, the Strollers recorded their highest total of the season, 155 runs. Hardy-King (31 not out) shared a record last wicket partnership of 39 with his friend, Frankie Mott, and Gozzett and Constantine bowled the gasmen out for 95 in the rain.

The following year, young Tom Gozzett joined his elder brother to spearhead the Strollers bowling attack. He makes no claim to great pace but his control of perfect length brought him immediate success in the helpful conditions that generally pertained. He recalls with very modest pride a newspaper headline declaring, 'Gozzett Brothers Take Ten Wickets'. The match he remembered was probably the one at Woodham Mortimer in 1936 that Strollers won by 13 runs. Joe Gozzett took seven for 18 and Tom three for 11 and the home side were dismissed for 43 runs.

Other games recalled from the 1930s include Birch Park and the local skirmishes with Maldon Town. Both Gozzett and Fenn smile at the recollection of playing at the Birch family seat of the Round family, who had been so influential in Essex cricket 70 years before. An air of sophistication pervaded the occasion with Major Round and military colleague Captain Crane featuring in the home side and being served tea by the family butler!

Maldon Town also preserved some vestiges of elitism. Being mostly traders of one sort or another, they played a number of mid-week matches as well as Saturdays. They would not play the Strollers on a Saturday, however, but only in a limited overs evening match. Tom and his contemporaries would not acknowledge that Maldon Town were any better a side, but they had an outstanding player in Jack Gower, although Tom commends him for his wicket-keeping skills, rather than confirming his reputation as a batsman.

One match was played between the Strollers and Town clubs on a Monday evening in June 1937. Strollers made 66 for four after losing three early wickets. Hardy-King hit 25 and Jiggins and Mott were undefeated on 21 and 16 respectively at the end of the overs. The Town made a disastrous reply, losing eight wickets for six runs to finish with a total of only 32, and the Gozzett brothers were nowhere to be seen. Kirby, with some of the 'best bowling in Maldon for a long while' took six wickets for seven runs and Jiggins and Pettit took two wickets apiece.

The Second World War put an end to another era of local cricket and, unfortunately, to Tom Gozzett's short career. When he left the Royal Air Force his health had suffered and he was unable to play again. Happily, though, he had married during the early years of the war and, in 1945, his son David was born to carry on the cricketing legacy and become an important figure in the formation of the new Maldon cricket club in 1976.

Cricket got back into its stride after the war and by 1948 there was again a full programme of fixtures. It was about this time, despite some rumblings from churchmen around the county, that Sunday cricket was widely introduced to satisfy the growing popularity of the game. Some argue, however, that Sunday cricket eventually undermined some local clubs, stretching both playing and organizational resources too thinly over two days. Maldon Strollers was flourishing and, despite the absence of captain, Len Hipsey through a footballing injury and vice-captain, Pat Bell who was out of the district, good teams were put into the field.

Deputising for the senior men, the team was led on the field by newcomer, Eddie Fisher, and old stalwart, Laurie Hardy-King. Fisher and Alec Hedgecock had joined the club from Great Baddow and Arthur Wordley had been recruited from Broomfield. Eighteen-year-old Phillip Gill also made his debut in 1948 – his older brothers, William, Hubert, Cliff, Alf, Edward and Tom had all played together for Heybridge when that club was in existence. During the season, Sid Boreham, the former captain of Langford joined the ranks and there were fleeting appearances by Mike Freeman and Arthur Moss.

Opposition was drawn from local village sides like Goldhanger, Wickham Bishops, Boreham and Great Totham, with trips further afield – despite petrol rationing – to Birch and Earls Colne. Of the local works sides, Bentalls were easily beaten in a Wednesday evening match, but the 'local derby' with Sadds was lost by three wickets in rain and bad light.

Overall, the season seems to have been a happy one, with the men losing a match for Maldon Carnival against the women of the club. In the tradition of such games, the men were handicapped by having to bowl, bat and field left-handed. To mark the end of the season a match between the Married and the Single was played for 50 bottles of beer that were

19. Maldon Strollers in 1950. Standing: (left to right) Tom Askew (umpire), Owen Wallis, Arthur Wordley, Eddie Fisher, George Crisp, Peter Radley, Mike Freeman and Les Fisher (scorer). Sitting: Geoff Gaunt, Roy Saville, Laurie Hardy-King (captain), Bill Pettit and Fred White.

consumed within 20 minutes of the end of the game! A dinner at the King's Head in December was attended by 50 people.

Among the jollity, however, the first signs of the serious problems that would beset Maldon cricket for the next 25 years began to show. The facilities at the Promenade were poor, the council giving little or no priority to the interests of local cricketers and creating disquiet over the future of the grounds at the Promenade. At their dinner in 1948, the Strollers members voiced their concerns about 'the uncertain position regarding the pavilion and wickets at the Prom', and in an expression of disgust at the care given by the council, they felt 'if the worst comes to the worst the club would have to play all away matches, rather than invite clubs to poor facilities'.

This extreme step was never taken. Laurie Hardy-King took over the captaincy from Eddie Fisher in 1950 and cricket for the Strollers continued through the decade despite the lack of any council expertise in pitch preparation. A new generation of young cricketers like Dave Gozzett, Keith Searle, Keith Bannister, Brian Cooper, Tim Baker and Brian Cutmore provided a new nucleus of players who were not prepared to accept the situation. Responsibility for cricket square maintenance was taken from the council by the club and improvement in the quality pitches, and of the cricket played on them, followed.

At about the same time – the mid-1960s – the Strollers agreed to share their ground with Maldonians, the club that grew from the Old Maldonians when they were displaced from the Grammar School ground. The relationship was often tense in the early days but as the clubs grew together and new personalities exercised a uniting influence, the basis for the new Maldon cricket club was established.

According to club folklore, the final portent for amalgamating the two clubs was the birth of a son to Dave and Sue Gozzett. The happy event occurred on the day that Strollers beat the Maldonians for the first time, creating the possibility of a marriage of equals. The young Gozzett, Marc, was later joined by three more brothers, all of whom played for the new Maldon cricket club: Marc and brother Steve remain active on and off the field today.

Chapter 25
Maldon Town's 'best ever season'

According to popular newspaper headlines, Maldon Town Cricket Club's best ever season was 1949. The town club was the direct descendent of the original Maldon club and included the names of Gower and Devenish, whose predecessors had played with distinction in the previous century. The downturn in fortunes at the start of the twentieth century had been outlived and Maldon Town had again been playing useful cricket on the local circuit since the early 1920s. That generation of cricketers, including the talented Jack Gower, had left the scene and the Second World War brought a tragic intermission in the local game.

By 1949 recovery was complete and cricket flourished all over the district in town, village, works and school. Great Braxted, who had disbanded when displaced from historic Braxted Park in the 1920s, reformed in 1949 having acquired the new ground in the village. In Maldon the Town club's premier status was challenged by the Strollers and the seeds of the Old Maldonians cricket club were sown. Bentalls and Sadds, the town's major employers provided playing fields for their works teams and all the clubs could display some good cricketers.

The Town club played on the Promenade, on the area subsequently lost to the bowling green and tennis courts. The Strollers occupied an adjoining area, where some of the minor Maldon games are played today. By all accounts, the Town had a far better service from the Council and Tony Gower, then an opening batsman, recalls pitches of the time as being good.

There was plenty of enthusiasm for cricket in the town and Sunday matches were becoming popular.

Arthur 'Stumpy' Moss was the new Town captain in 1949. He was a talented and inventive left-handed batsman and could bowl either seam or spin. He nursed ambitions as a professional footballer and the other game caused him to miss the occasional early or late season game of cricket. Unlike today, however, it was entirely possible for both games to be seriously pursued at a high level. Tony Gower was vice-captain and the established nucleus of the side was completed by Basil Smart, John Devenish, Stan Clarke, Les Wager and Dick Filby. Young schoolboys like Geoff Newman, Peter Vince and Mike Freeman also began to appear in senior cricket at this time.

The season began badly with losses to Coggeshall, Stock, Hatfield Peverel and Crittalls before fortunes turned for the better. A resounding win over Royal Army Service Corps at Colchester began a run of wins against Earls Colne, Maldon Strollers, the Warren and works clubs, Mildmay Ironworks and Christy' Sports. By August the Town had won seven of their last eight games.

The derby match against the Strollers was a low scoring affair in which John Devenish (six for 15) and Basil Smart (four for 13) routed Strollers for 38, Pip Gill only reaching double figures on 11 not out. Town batting first had not done much better, Gower's 18 being the only significant contribution to the total of 58. Wordley took four Town wickets for 13 and Hedgecock three for 20. The more keenly fought derby match of the year was against Mildmay Ironworks, played on the Sunday of the August bank holiday weekend. Maldon won after scoring 144 for nine declared after a good opening stand by Gower (34) and Clarke (20) and 41 from Devenish. With the Burnham side at 130 for five at the close it was agreed to extend time to achieve a result. Mildmay lost their last five wickets for five runs and Maldon won by nine. The weekend was a personal triumph for John Devenish who scored an almost unheard of total of 172 runs in the three matches played.

Runs were also flowing in the return match with Stock when Maldon scored a rare total of over 200 runs. The Town won by 67 runs, with young Michael Dowsett, then on leave from National Service, taking five for 46, as Stock were dismissed for 162. The return match with Hatfield Peverel was not so successful. Facing a total of 130-6 declared, Maldon were bundled out for 33, their lowest total of the season. 'Snowy' Bright and 'Curly' Willsher took five Maldon wickets apiece.

Similarly, the Town was no match for a Witham side in a late season match. Maldon was dismissed for 40, chasing a total of 201 for eight declared. The club also struggled against Coggeshall, demonstrating that, generally, it did not have the strength in depth that the bigger clubs could command. In Arthur Moss and John Devenish, Maldon had two very gifted all-round cricketers but, if their availability or form suffered, the competence of the team as a whole diminished. Moss scored 600 runs in 1949, a massive haul for the time despite missing several games, and was usually among the wickets. He was a confident player, whose readiness to improvise to score runs was based on good technique. His departure to play for Hatfield Peverel in 1950 was a bitter blow.

The reasons for Moss's departure cannot be fully known, but the uncertainty created by the council's proposals for the Promenade cannot have helped the Town club's peace of mind. At the same time as the Strollers were contemplating departure from the ground because of the unacceptably poor facilities, the Town were facing expulsion because of plans to relocate the bowling club from London Road.

Despite the problems, plenty of young players came into the club, principally through the Grammar School that had strong cricket traditions and good facilities. In addition to those already mentioned, Graham Mott, John Hill, Terry Moss and his brothers were among those who represented Maldon in the 1950s. By then, the playing field off Fambridge Road had been purchased by the Maldon Town Social & Athletic Club in an ambitious scheme to create a centre for sport in Maldon.

20. Maldon Town in 1948. Standing: (left to right) Joe Wendon, Les Wager, John Devenish, Basil Smart, Tony Gower, Les Drain. Sitting: Stan Baker, Ron Reidling, Stan Clarke, Geoff Newman, Mike Freeman and Arthur Moss.

Unfortunately the ambitions for cricket did not materialise and, while the Town club began playing there in the mid-1950s, the playing facilities never reached the standard required for good club cricket.

Enthusiasm eventually waned and it became increasingly difficult to meet playing commitments. The Social & Athletic Club was dominated by the interests of Maldon Town football that commanded by far the greater public interest at the time. In about 1958, 200 years after their forebears trudged with bat and ball to play cricket on Potman Marsh, the Maldon club disbanded and the players went their separate ways to other clubs or retirement. Fortunately, the Old Maldonians club was in the ascendancy and attracted some of the best players who lived on to see the merger with the Strollers club that led to the new Maldon cricket club taking the field in 1976.

Chapter 26

Geoff Newman: 50 years in Maldon cricket

Through the lives of two men, living more than 100 years apart, it is possible to see the major developments in Maldon cricket during the nineteenth and twentieth centuries. Thomas Tomlinson (see Chapter 13) played in the great Maldon teams of the 1800s and Geoff Newman lived through the many changes of more recent times. In 1996, he celebrated 50 years as a Maldon cricketer. This chapter is based on conversations with him.

Tomlinson and Newman were more than just cricketers. They took responsibility for the leadership of their clubs, on the field and off it. Both men held the important honorary positions within their clubs but their part in promoting the reputation of those clubs was much greater than any posts they may have held. Under Tomlinson, Maldon grew in Essex cricket circles from good club at Potman Marsh to great club at the Fairfield. Newman's times were more turbulent but he worked ceaselessly to establish Maldon's credentials despite the problems confronting the local game after the Second World War.

Geoff Newman arrived in Maldon in 1944 with a passion for sport and ability enough to establish a reputation for table tennis and soccer, as well as cricket. He came to live in Park Drive, which runs beside Maldon's Promenade where both the Town and the Strollers clubs had their grounds at that time. As was invariably the case in days when youngsters had to make their own way in the world, it was left to Geoff to loiter at the evening net sessions, waiting for an invitation to participate and, perhaps, to make up the numbers in a club match. His opportunity soon came along and he found himself playing during the school holidays for the Maldon Town Wednesday Eleven.

Meanwhile, at the Grammar School where the traditional values of cricket were revered, Newman, after performing well for the under-13s against other schools, including Braintree Grammar School, was selected for the First Eleven at the unusually young age of 14. The facilities and coaching at the School were excellent under the influence of Mr Williams, who had also established something of a reputation for youth cricket with the Essex county club. By the age of 15, Newman had established a regular place in the Maldon Town club's weekend team, although not as a 'young fast bowler with natural away swing' that he reckoned himself to be.

In those days you had to wait for your opportunities and Maldon Town, with John Devenish, Basil Smart and Arthur Moss, were well endowed with bowlers. Undaunted, Geoff declared himself to be a wicketkeeper so that he could stay at the centre of the action and study the senior bowlers at close quarters. He was also developing his abilities with the bat, often impressing when established players had failed.

Reminiscing about the old times when cars were a luxury and petrol was rationed, Geoff remembers the problems encountered travelling to away games. For local trips a builder's lorry was often used with straw bales in the back serving as makeshift seats for the players. The old Moore's bus that trundled the long route to Chelmsford would be used for trips to Hatfield Peverel, with the club bag stowed under the steel stairway to the upper deck. The club bag then contained all the pads, gloves, boxes and bats needed for a game: some players might own a bat but all other equipment was provided by the club.

Coaches were occasionally hired for longer journeys and the team and its entourage always travelled to Burnham by coach for the annual bank holiday clash with Mildmay

Ironworks. When playing the match at the Promenade, spectators would arrive early with their chairs to reserve the best positions to watch the clash between such favourites as Gordon Brasted for the visitors and Maldon's local hero, John 'the Kaiser' Devenish.

On one occasion at Burnham, Devenish remonstrated with Brasted who had delivered a short pitched ball that narrowly missed his nose. Bouncers in those days were not considered entirely proper and the Kaiser requested, 'Would you mind pitching it up, young man?' Brasted responded with an attempted fast yorker that fell short of its intended length, whereupon Devenish's mighty bat swung through its arc and the ball sailed from the ground, over the road and disappeared through the window of an unlucky shopkeeper!

Pitches in the late 1940s were generally poor, although the Town's home pitch was still reasonable and good tracks were often produced at Southminster. At Runwell Hospital, where a notorious fast bowler called Brown played, an apocryphal story has a ball pitching, flying over both batsman and wicketkeeper and clearing the boundary before it pitched again! At Tiptree, coconut matting was laid on the Chapel Road football pitch, while at Goldhanger, matting was laid on concrete. If changing facilities existed at all, they would be unserviced shacks. Usually privacy was sought from the cover of bushes or whatever vehicles had brought the team to the ground.

In the early 1950s, the Town club were obliged to vacate the Promenade to enable the new bowling green and tennis courts to be built. Several seasons as a wandering club followed before a new home was found at the Maldon Town Social & Athletic Club's new ground off Fambridge Road. Throughout these problem years Newman stayed loyal to the Town club but, by 1956, he was convinced that cricket would always be the poor relation in the sharing arrangement at the new ground. Pitches were poorly prepared and, as the success of Maldon Town Football Club grew, little thought was given to the needs of good club cricket. He threw in his lot with the recently established Old Maldonians cricket club and was joined, a couple of years later, by several of his colleagues when the Town club finally folded.

In 1955 Geoff was asked to act as vice-captain of the Maldon & District Eleven that played the MCC to mark the bicentenary of cricket in the town (see chapter 29). Celebrating another milestone 25 years later, he skippered the new Maldon cricket club in the 1980 match against the Essex county cricket club (see chapter 31).

By then, Geoff Newman had played an important part in building the reputation of the Old Maldonians club as a disciplined and competent team on the local circuit. Few matches were lost under his leadership on the field and his careful brand of self-confessed 'benevolent dictatorship' between matches always ensured the team was well turned out and organized. Throughout the 1960s, fixtures improved, team morale developed and the club looked towards rebuilding itself to match the bigger clubs.

In the event, that objective was achieved through partnership with Maldon Strollers, when they joined with the then styled Maldonians to form the new Maldon cricket club in 1976. A few years later the future status of the club was secured when the cricket facilities at Drapers Farm were successfully developed. Newman remembers the hard work done by the likes of Jim Lionnel, Brian Strudwick, Brian Cutmore and Dave Gozzett from the former Strollers club during this crucial phase in the building of the new club.

For the first 14 years of its new found existence, Newman served as club captain at Maldon and as captain of the Second Eleven, with which he achieved enormous success in the Two Counties Second Eleven Competition. In his veteran years, his energies were channelled more and more into Two Counties cricket and for many years now he has run the heavily subscribed Over-50s representative eleven.

Once or twice he has been spotted on the field since his official retirement in 1996 after 50 years as a Maldon cricketer.

He can invariably be found, however, at all of Maldon's East Anglian Premier League matches, often speculating how the players of his day might have fared at this rarefied level of the game. In recent years, he opines, Maldon have produced two outstanding young cricketers in Alastair Cook and David Randall but generally, the best players of the past would still be the best players today, *if* they had the opportunities, the coaching, the facilities and the structure for progression that today's club players take for granted.

Like most of his generation Geoff Newman rues the intrusion of 'cheque-book cricket' into the game that for generations prided itself on the amateur spirit of it recreational arm. He accepts philosophically, however, that that is the price to be paid for the return of the very best club cricket to Maldon, an aim to which he has dedicated much of his own leisure time.

Chapter 27

Old Maldonians Cricket Club

The Grammar School at Maldon was an institution dating back to the seventeenth century before it was swept away by the educational reforms of the 1960s. Originally the school was held at the St Peter's church building (now the Maeldune Centre) before finding larger premises in London Road. After education became the responsibility of the newly formed Essex County Council, a new grammar school and teacher training centre was built at Fambridge Road and that building forms the red brick core of the Upper Plume School today.

Ex-pupils of the grammar school became know as 'Old Maldonians' and, in the nineteenth century, an Old Maldonians Association was formed. Although the school aped some of the traditions of the famous public schools, it remained a strictly local seat of learning, providing classes in literacy, numeracy and religious understanding sufficient to prepare pupils for the many white collar jobs in Maldon's growing factories. While the children of wealthy families went away to boarding school, the growing middle-class stratum of old Maldonians began to exercise an influence on local affairs.

As well as the study of formal subjects the grammar school had always promoted games, including cricket, although this must have been somewhat difficult without a playing field. When the school played the Old Maldonians (the first reference to such a team) in 1905, the match was staged at the Fairfield, home of the Maldon club. The game was a feature of the annual gathering of the Old Maldonians Association that culminated with dinner at the King's Head. The two innings match was won by the 'Old Boys' by eight wickets.

In 1907, the Old Maldonians Association dinner was held at the Blue Boar that had become the natural meeting place for Maldon's men of commerce. That year the new grammar school opened on the site at the northern end of the Fairfield that presumably became a recreational area for the school. The cricket club had played their matches there since 1848 but, by the time the new school opened, it was teetering on the brink of obscurity.

Initially, the new school ran into difficulties, not least from the moral outrage following news that the teacher training facility was to be mixed sex. The problem of low student numbers was paradoxically solved by allowing entry to girl pupils and, by the 1920s, the school had settled into the role of educating the sons and daughters of the respectable middle-classes of Maldon and district. Conscious efforts were made to retain links between the school and its former pupils and one vehicle for this was the annual cricket match between Old Maldonians and School teams, a tradition that survived until comprehensive education.

The annual match spawned the idea of a permanent cricket section of the Old Maldonians Association and by the 1950s, the Old Maldonians cricket club added its presence to the several clubs playing in the town. Claud Rayner, who captained the Old Maldonians in 1956, recalls playing against Colchester Nomads in what he believes was the new club's first full season in 1951. Home matches were played on the old Fairfield, or the grammar school playing field as it had become, and the team was led by Mike Brewer, who has, for reasons unknown always had the nickname, 'Buzz'.

Records confirm that Old Maldonians did play against Colchester Nomads on 30 June 1951, and won by 51 runs. Brewer made 43 not out, Michael Dowsett 43 and Keith Ballentyne 21 out of a total of 142 runs for seven wickets declared, made off 37 overs. Ray Bongard, a fast and hostile bowler, then took seven wickets for 32 runs as the Nomads replied with 91 runs all out. Ten matches were played that year, including one against Maldon Town that was abandoned with the Old Maldonians score at 29 runs for three wickets, chasing the Town total of 104.

Buzz Brewer, whose son, the tall off spinner, Derek, took the new Maldon club's bowler of the year award in 1992, topped the batting averages in 1951 with 233 runs from six completed innings. Keith Ballentyne was second with an average of 21 and Michael Dowsett third with 14 runs per innings completed. Ray Bongard was the leading wicket taker with 20 at an average of 10.7 but Brian Mills topped the averages with 12 wickets at nine runs apiece. Brewer took five wickets at 8.8, but he shared wicket-keeping duties with Rayner and also took six catches and three stumpings.

The club began to prosper throughout the 1950s on the local cricket circuit. Strong links were maintained with the grammar school, where cricket was a passion among several of the senior masters, who hoped that top club cricket could be brought back to Maldon. The school ground provided good facilities and several of the younger teachers played for the club, although Jim Harrison, a gifted cricketer from Staffordshire, after a few outings at Maldon, moved to play at Hatfield Peverel, where several other capable newcomers to the town also chose to play. Harrison, however, progressed to the then top level with Chelmsford cricket club, before returning to his native county and ultimately emigrating to Australia.

A boost to the strength of the Old Maldonians occurred when the Maldon Town club folded in the late 1950s. Geoff Newman had decamped in 1956, to be joined a couple of years later by Tony Gower and Graham Mott, whose contrasting batting styles provided a reliable opening partnership into the 1960s. Membership was, however, still restricted to those who had attended the grammar school and this prevented other fine players joining from the defunct Town club. Had both the Moss brother, Terry – an outstanding schoolboy cricketer – and Roy, been at the school, their abilities may well have taken the improving side to a higher level. As it was, they chose to play together for Crittalls at Witham Park.

Open membership was not too far in the future when the early plans for comprehensive education were published. Several of the teachers at the school who had been most interested in cricket retired and a more radical attitude emerged within the club itself. By the early 1960s the school facilities were withdrawn and, as the other two Maldon clubs had before it, the Old Maldonians experienced a period as a wandering club. Playing strength, however, improved. The nucleus of established players that included, Peter Vince, one of the most naturally talented cricketers in the district, was expanded to include young Nigel Patten, who had represented Nottingham University as an opening batsman.

In severing the final links with the grammar school, the club threw open its membership and sought, with partial success, to recruit players from other local clubs. In 1965, the Old Maldonians began a sharing arrangement on the Promenade ground with the Strollers club but, behind the scenes, the first seeds of an ambitious plan to buy a new ground were sown. In 1973 the club restyled itself 'Maldonians' in a further effort to rid itself of the 'old boys' image and fund raising for a new ground went public. Among a raft of ideas from entrepreneur, Albert Wright, then landlord of the Chequers, was one for a smoking concert.

How times had changed since the cricket club's members had enjoyed their pipes and some traditional songs at the White Horse smoking concert in 1907. The one at the Swan in the 1970s featured a particularly blue ventriloquist and a quartet of obliging East End ladies removing their clothes. Such an event had never been held in Maldon before and the local police were nervous at the prospective offence against public decency. The club assured the law that the concert was for members only and overnight recruited 200 new members!

21. Derby Day on the Promenade in the 1960s. A ball from Brian Cutmore of Maldon Strollers beats Old Maldonians' Geoff Newman and is taken by wicketkeeper Robbie Hyde. Prolific opening batsman, Nigel Patten, is the non-striker and the field appears to be an attacking one!

Back on the cricket field, the new generation of players included those like Colin Philpott, Peter Manning, Eric Hawkridge, Glyn Webster and Tony White, who would be prime movers in the formation of the new Maldon cricket club. The Strollers were strengthened by players like Maldon football manager, Kevin Barron, a rejuvenated Arthur Moss, who had captained the Town club in 1949, and newcomer Jim Lionnel. When it became clear that no landowners would release land for a cricket ground because of the massive price inflation from the housing boom, talks began, surreptitiously at first, about a possible merger of the two clubs.

The idea took root and was raised formally a couple of years later. In 1975, both clubs took resolutions to their annual meetings and agreed to the formation of the new Maldon cricket club the following year.

Chapter 28

Maldon & District Cricket Association

The Maldon & District Cricket Association played its first match on 10 September 1949, against the Essex county cricket club. The Association was the brainchild of Mr E. M. Williams, a classics master at the grammar school, who had a passion for cricket and sought ceaselessly to impress upon the boys the importance of a straight bat, in life as well as in cricket.

He had been at the school since the First World War and was active in youth cricket for the Essex county club, with which he enjoyed strong connections. Peter Smith, the Essex leg spin bowler who had toured Australia and New Zealand with England in 1946/47, was particularly close and visited Maldon several times in 1949. In April, he gave a talk to the cricketers of Bentalls at the Headquarters building at Heybridge (now sadly demolished) and, during the summer term, he came to coach the School's First Eleven.

The formation of the Association was a move to bring together a strong local side that could attract top clubs back to Maldon. Cricket at the school had a high priority and the square was meticulously maintained by the groundsman under the beady eyes of some of the senior masters. It must have been frustrating for them to see young players of real ability leave the school and distribute their talents among the numerous local clubs, rather than stay together to form a strong club team. Although boys living in the town may have graduated to the Town club, an equal number joined the ranks of their village team.

At least this meant that Monty Williams had a strong network of contacts within local clubs to assist his idea of a local Association. He had no difficulty recruiting all but a few of the local teams with the prospect of a representative match against Essex County Cricket Club, doubtless arranged through the good offices of Peter Smith. Many names were put forward and the final selection process was left to a panel under the chairmanship of another grammar school teacher, Stanley Anderson. Mr T. Askew was vice-chairman.

In order to see the contenders in action, a trial match was organized in August to assist with final selection. The following list of trialists gives a good account of the leading cricketers of the time and how they were distributed around the district. They were:

Eyre and Willsher of Hatfield Peverel
Dowsett and Romain of Maldon Grammar School
Frost and Moss of Great Braxted
Mann and Pook of Great Totham
Diaper, Gower and Ponder of Tolleshunt D'Arcy
Moss, Clark and Smart of Maldon Town
Hill of Bentalls
Atkins, Glassborrow and Jewitt of Latchingdon
Radley and Wordley of Maldon Strollers
Parker of Old Maldonians
Vince, Wallis and Wakefield of Sadds

After a late change of venue from the Promenade, the trial match was played on Sadds sports field, off the Causeway, on Sunday, 7 August. Arthur Moss of Maldon Town had to withdraw because professional football commitments would have prevented his appearance in the final match and Cyril Wakefield of Sadds was unable to appear. One new face, Eddie Fisher of Maldon Strollers, was drafted in and his performance impressed sufficiently to secure his inclusion in the final eleven.

Peter Smith duly captained the Essex Eleven and was joined by his cousin Ray, who played 419 times for Essex and was about to embark on the Commonwealth tour of India, Ceylon and Pakistan in the winter of 1949/50. Unfortunately for the Maldon bowlers, the team also included 'Dicky' Dodds and 'Sonny' Avery, the county's opening pair, who together scored nearly 35,000 runs for Essex between 1935 and 1959. At the time they were at the height of their powers and notorious for their ability to destroy the best bowling on the first-class circuit.

So it was that the pair punished the local bowlers to the tune of 150 in a crowd pleasing opening partnership of which Dodds, always the more cavalier, made 98 and Avery 52. There was no respite for Maldon as Stan Cray (77), Bill Dines (54) and Richard Horsfall (59 not out), all county players in their prime, piled on the runs. Smith finally declared at tea when the Essex total was an unassailable 404 runs for seven wickets.

The Maldon response was a miserable one. Mann made 32, Willsher 20 and Eyre 17 but, after Ray Smith had taken three wickets for 42 runs, all the Essex players, except wicketkeeper, Tommy Wade, took turns to have a bowl. Parker enlivened the dying stages of the game by striking four sixes and four fours in an innings of 47 runs, but his efforts only boosted the score to 165 all out. The Maldon & District Cricket Association were beaten all too easily by 239 runs and the gulf between the county men and their local counterparts was clearly exposed.

Whether Monty Williams expected a more encouraging performance from his protégées is not clear but he was certainly dissuaded from pressing ahead with further matches for the representative eleven. No other games are recorded until the outing against the MCC six years later (see chapter 29) to mark the bicentenary of cricket in Maldon.

Instead, he and other schoolmasters, including Stanley Anderson, Wilfred Berridge and Harry Bream, gave their support to creating a cricket section of the Old Maldonians Association (see chapter 27). The Town club was beginning to experience difficulties with the loss of its ground on the Promenade and perhaps the best young cricketers from the school could be channelled into an old boys club that could continue to enjoy the facilities, the traditions and the camaraderie of the school. Perhaps a new club could be built around them to challenge the supremacy of the Chelmsfords, Brentwoods and Colchesters on the county club circuit.

Perhaps the initiative was 20 years too late. Time was catching up with the men involved, old-fashioned values were being challenged and the nature of education was about to receive a severe shock to its system.

Chapter 29

Bicentenary match versus MCC 1955

To celebrate 200 years of cricket since the challenges of 1755 a match was played at Maldon against the MCC on 27 July 1955. This was the second outing for the Maldon & District Cricket Association that had played their inaugural game against the Essex county cricket club in 1949. School teacher, E. M. Williams, was again the organizer and, to commemorate the anniversary, he published a booklet entitled *Cricket: A Bicentenary in an Essex Setting.*

The booklet describes the challenge issued by Thomas Brand and muses about how an early match on Potman Marsh might have been conducted. Williams also suggests that a match was played, on 15 July 1755, as a result of the challenge although no source reference is given and no supporting evidence for the suggestion has come to light during my researches. Whether or not a match was played has no bearing on the historical integrity of the bicentenary celebration, as both Brand and Edwick made it clear in their public notices that a cricket club existed at Maldon in 1755.

The team selected for the 1955 match against the MCC was:

Dr J. Warren and J. Holmes of Southminster
C. Collins and A. Kemp of Tillingham
A. Moss and E. Willsher of Hatfield Peverel
L. Wash of Tollesbury
P. Vince of Old Maldonians
A. Cochrane and B. Mutter of the Warren

22. Maldon & District versus the MCC 1955. Mr E. M. Williams stands behind T. N. Pearce (with Mayor Tonkin) on the Grammar School steps with the players in the bicentenary match. Geoff Newman stands on the extreme left, shoulder to shoulder with Peter Vince, with Charlie Collins, Tillingham's classy batsman between them.

G. Newman of Maldon Town
Twelfth men: C. Arthy of Hatfield Peverel, G. Brasted of Mildmay Ironworks and J. Joslin of Terling.

The captain was Dr Warren of Southminster and the vice-captain was Geoff Newman of Maldon Town. Mr A. T. Blackwell was the appointed umpire and Mr Saffen, the scorer.

Looking back to the match against Essex in 1949, that Maldon & District lost so heavily, it can be seen that only two players from the 24 trialists for the earlier match were included in the 1955 team. They were Willsher of Hatfield Peverel and Moss, the former Maldon Town captain, who had also moved to Hatfield Peverel.

Suitably, the venue for the match was the Maldon Grammar School ground, the site of the old Fairfield that had witnessed the Maldon club's great matches during the previous century.

Also appropriately, the MCC was led by T. N. Pearce, a former pupil of the school. By 1955, Pearce had retired from the Essex captaincy and was chairman of the club, for whom he had played 231 times. He would later become the long-standing president of Essex County Cricket Club.

Other Essex players on display were W. G. Spencer, who played occasionally between 1938 and 1948; A. B. Quick, who played 19 matches at about that time and became Essex chairman in 1976, and the Unwin brothers. Frederick Unwin played 52 first-class matches between 1932 and 1950 and was joint captain of Essex in 1939. His brother, Ernest Unwin, played only a few first-class cricket matches but he did tour South Africa with the British Lions rugby team in 1938.

It was the Unwin brothers who rebuilt the MCC innings after Kemp and Willsher had taken three early wickets. Frederick, dropped by Newman when he had scored eight, went on to play a major innings, but Ernest, was bowled by Brasted for 48, giving the MCC a total of 170 runs for four wickets at lunch. Immediately after lunch Willsher took the wickets of Quick and Rankin with successive balls, but Maldon was unable to press home their advantage against a resilient lower order. Holmes was eventually rewarded with the wicket of Pearce, who declared the innings closed at a total of 264 runs for nine wickets.

Unfortunately, the full scorecard for the match has not survived and details of the Maldon & District innings are sketchy, but with a closing score of 164 for seven wickets, an honourable draw was achieved. Newman recalls going in at number eight with Monty Williams' instructions ringing in his ears, 'Play up and down the line and don't get out!' The 21-year-old dasher obeyed and played out time, despite sage advice from the professionals surrounding his bat to 'play a few shots!'

This match was much more closely contested than that with Essex in 1949 when the District team was clearly outclassed. The fall of early wickets gave the MCC men food for thought and the double breakthrough after lunch brought Maldon back into the game. But old professionals will always have some inner reserves to call upon and, generally, their bowling is too straight for their club counterparts.

Williams did not proceed with the idea of further District XI matches to bring a higher standard of cricket back to Maldon. Although most of the local clubs readily affiliated to the Maldon & District Cricket Association, their first loyalty was to their own clubs. By the mid-1950s, the Old Maldonians cricket club had been established and it was thought it could grow strong by offering club cricket to ex-pupils who had developed through the Grammar School's excellent facilities.

Part 6

The New Maldon Cricket Club

Chapter 30
The phoenix rises

When, following a difficult few years after leaving the Promenade, the Maldon Town club wound up in 1958, the history of the great club that had waxed and waned for 200 years came to an end. By 1960 the two main cricket clubs in the town were Maldon Strollers and Old Maldonians. Unsurprisingly, there were deep rivalries and clashes of values between them. The schools system that divided children by the 'eleven-plus' examination, was effectively being perpetuated into the sporting and social life of the town.

Fortunately, times were changing and, by 1965 when the Old Maldonians began sharing the Strollers' ground, all significant ties with the former grammar school had been severed. But the old boy's stigma remained and, for several years, the atmosphere between the clubs as they prepared their pitches and played their games on the same square, was not always easy. Gradually, the workers in the respective clubs became used to each other and, when two useful cricketers, Jim Lionnel and Tony White, moved into Maldon they became the catalysts that were needed for final change.

Both men joined the Strollers club but Tony defected to the Maldonians after a season or two; Jim stayed loyal but played and drank with the Maldonians whenever he could. More importantly, as newcomers, they were able to speak openly about the absurdity of the arrangements between the clubs and the advantages of a merger. By the early 1970s the possibility was an open secret and there was even a sit down meeting between officials of the two clubs on neutral territory at the King's Head.

Naturally there was resistance to the idea in both camps, but the people running the clubs could not ignore the advantages. The problems they faced were rooted in lack of volunteers and lack of money. Firstly, with Saturday and Sunday cricket, it was often difficult to find eleven players. Secondly, having taken over maintenance of the square from the council, the same few individuals were relied upon to repair and prepare pitches for weekend matches. Overriding everything was the problem of finance: ground maintenance machinery was expensive to maintain, let alone to buy.

Pooling resources was the perfect answer to these problems and eventually common sense prevailed. In 1975, proposals were prepared for the annual meetings of both clubs who duly agreed to amalgamate and play under the title of 'Maldon Cricket Club'. An inaugural meeting was held at the Ship & Anchor on 1 October and the new club prepared to take the field for the first time in 1976.

If the process seemed to work smoothly, this was thanks only to the careful hard work behind the scenes by members of both clubs. A small working party had been responsible for drawing up detailed proposals, a constitution and plans for the first season. Sue Manning, who later became club president, acted as its secretary and Colin Philpott, who subsequently served as club chairman for 22 years, co-ordinated affairs. Other prime movers were David Gozzett, Brian Strudwick, Peter Manning and the late Tony White. The first officials appointed to the new Maldon club were:

President:	Ron Harris
Vice-presidents:	Tony Gower and Claud Rayner
Chairman:	Colin Philpott
Vice-chairman:	Brian Strudwick
Secretary:	Sue Manning
Treasurer:	Dave Gozzett
Fixtures secretary:	Tony White (assisted by Tim Baker)

Care was taken to share influence in the new club between key members of the old, but one issue – captaincy – proved too

23. Architects of the new Maldon cricket club? Many of the members behind the generation of the new club came together in 1987 to win a local veterans knockout competition. Several are still influential today.

Left to right: Mick Bardo, Tony Marchi, John Hill, John Cloake, Robbie Hyde, John Ellis, Mick Martin, Bob Barnes, Geoff Newman, Colin Philpott and Chris Elliott.

hot for the inaugural meeting to handle. Much of the good work done to form the new club could have been unravelled by insensitive captaincy on the field, so the answer was to do nothing. With a starting balance of £240 the club had no immediate money worries and the annual subscription was fixed at £1. Match fees were 25p. In the best tradition, members celebrated their new deal with a social evening at the Great Eastern Railway Tavern on 17 October.

The first season of 1976 succeeded in cementing the new club together. League cricket lay some way in the future so the programme of matches was a continuation of the fixtures of the former clubs. Teams were picked to reflect the strength of the opposition and acting captains were appointed from week to week. Over the season 52 players represented the club in 63 matches, 29 of which were won. There were inevitably some grumbles from players who felt their talents were not being fully used and from those whose treatment suffered from the inconsistencies of shared captaincy. Some players drifted from the scene but, generally, the club had got off to a solid start.

By the middle of the second season, the determination of the players to make the new club successful was being overtaken by the frustrations arising from split strength teams and shared captaincy. In order to get some clearer policies in place a requisition for an extraordinary meeting of the club was supported by John Cloake, Brian Cutmore, Eric Hawkridge, Geoff Newman and the late Peter Sarling. The extraordinary meeting was held on Sunday, 10 July 1977 at the Queen Victoria, when, without serious dissent, the club decided to select teams strictly on ability for the 1978 season.

Glyn Webster, a tireless worker for Maldon cricket until he moved to Norfolk, was appointed match secretary to implement the new arrangements, which proved highly effective. The club could at last demonstrate the strength of its first eleven that was now being infiltrated by a clutch of talented youngsters coming through the system. New players were attracted, notably Chris Elliott, who, threw his substantial talents and energies into the club in 1978.

By 1979 the new club was well established and ready to move forward. Peter Manning had emerged as the regular first eleven captain and the minds of the members had turned to the burning issue of league cricket. Of far greater significance, however, were the discussions beginning with the council about a new sports ground at Drapers Farm, Heybridge.

Chapter 31

Versus Essex County Cricket Club 1980

The new Maldon club's first exposure to cricketing celebrity came in 1980, to celebrate 225 years since the challenges of 1755. A team representing Essex County Cricket Club came to play at the Promenade on Sunday, 21 September.

The Essex team was led by veteran Brian Taylor, who had been captain of the county for six years until his retirement in 1973. Taylor had made one tour with England to South Africa in 1956/57 and later became a test selector. Graham Saville had also retired after 11 years with Essex and was on his way to becoming one of the country's best respected coaches as a result of his work with the England under-19 squad. He would later prove a thorn in the Maldon team's side as an opening batsman for the Braintree club.

Most of the county's team consisted of young players who would progress to leave their mark on the first-class game. Paul Prichard, at just 15 years of age, had already been spotted as one of the best young batsman around and Neil Foster, at 17, had been called from his school studies to make his Essex debut in 1980. Prichard made his debut for Essex in 1984 and became captain on the retirement of Graham Gooch. Foster, despite serious injury that interrupted his career, developed into a lively new ball bowler for England.

Both men later became friends of the Maldon club, enjoying benefit matches hosted at Drapers Farm in 1993 and 1996. Paul Prichard, who also played occasionally when recovering from injury, remains a vice-president today, while Neil Foster was the club coach who assisted the powerful team of 2003 to finish runner-up in the East Anglian Premier League.

Others who represented Essex were Chris Gladwin, Ian Pont and Gary Sainsbury. Gladwin, who was promising enough to open the batting with Gooch for a time left Essex in 1987 and finished his first class career with Derbyshire in 1989. Later he was encountered on the Two Counties circuit playing for Bury Rail. Pont went first to Nottinghamshire in 1982 before returning to Essex for three years, but his all round talents could not command a regular first team place. He went to America to trial as a baseball pitcher but he too eventually returned to Two Counties cricket with Witham. Sainsbury, a left arm medium fast bowler, had already made the first-class team in 1980 but later moved to spend five years with Gloucestershire. One other young player, Martin Olley, failed to make the Essex first team but made appearances for both Northamptonshire and Middlesex during the 1980s.

Maldon club captain, Geoff Newman, took charge of the home team on a bright and sunny day on a Promenade ground that had been manicured to look its best. The pitch, however, had been shaved of grass and proved too slow for the stroke playing visitors: Prichard had time for a smile as he waited for the first ball of the match to reach his bat from the pitch. Eventually he was caught behind the wicket by Hyde off Webster but it was Hawkridge's accurate medium pace that was testing the patience, of which Gladwin proved to have very little. It was left to Saville to see the Essex team to a respectable total with the assistance of a fifty from Gouldstone, as Manning removed the middle order.

It was different for Elliott and Philpott opening the Maldon innings against Foster and Sainsbury. More than once, the harassed 'Runs' was heard to mutter 'too good for me mate!' After the opening burst had removed the pair, Taylor resorted to his second string bowlers who allowed most of the order to have a few runs. Brian Hughes, later ground manager at Chelmsford, enticed some errors and Saville's experimental leg

24. Maldon versus Essex County Cricket Club 1980. Top row: K. Shoemake, C. Gladwin, D. Gozzett, N. Hilliard, C. Elliott, N. Foster, D. Newton, I. Pont, D. Raymond, M. Gouldstone, P. Manning, M. Olley, B. Hughes. Bottom row: C. Philpott, R. Hyde, G. Sainsbury, G. Rayner, B. Taylor, G. Newman, G. Saville, E. Hawkridge, P. Prichard, G. Webster.

Maldon versus an Essex XI: Sunday, 21 September 1980

Essex			
P. Prichard	c. Hyde	b. Webster	18
M. Gouldstone		b. Manning	52
C. Gladwin	c. Newman	b. Hawkridge	2
N. Hilliard	c. & b.	b. Rayner	10
G. Saville	c. Gozzett	b. Manning	79
I. Pont	c. Rayner	b. Manning	2
M. Olley	not out		0
N. Foster	c. Newman	b. Hawkridge	6
G. Sainsbury	c. Hawkridge	b. Manning	0
B. Hughes	did not bat		
B. Taylor	did not bat		
Extras			5
	Total (for 8 wickets declared)		**174**

Maldon			
C. Philpott		b. Foster	10
C. Elliott		b. Sainsbury	13
D. Raymond	c. Olley	b. Hughes	22
K. Shoemake		b. Gladwin	5
D. Gozzett		b. Saville	3
G. Rayner	st. Olley	b. Hughes	21
G. Newman	c. & b.	b. Hughes	6
P. Manning	c. Taylor	b. Hughes	27
G. Webster	not out		18
R. Hyde		b. Pont	1
E. Hawkridge	not out		1
Extras			15
	Total (for 9 wickets)		**142**

Match drawn

breaks conceded some runs. In the end the game was saved by Maldon who were still 32 runs away from victory with the last pair together.

It was a highly enjoyable day that began to establish the friendly and hospitable reputation of the new Maldon club. Later in the decade, with a new ground at Drapers Farm and new status in the Two Counties Championship, the Maldon clubhouse would become a popular haunt of many cricketers seeking refuge from the rigours of first-class play.

Chapter 32

Two Counties Championship

By the time the new Maldon club had settled down, the big issue facing local clubs was league cricket. There were those that continued to oppose the trend on the grounds that the sporting ethos of the game would be the first casualty of greater competitiveness; others argued that leagues were the only way forward and clubs who buried their heads in the sand would be sidelined and lose their best players.

Such arguments raged at Maldon, with traditionalists supporting existing arrangements and newcomers and younger players wanting to enter a league. The argument could not run indefinitely. Although leagues had come and gone in most parts of Essex over the years, their time seemed have finally arrived in the 1970s. Already, good fixtures were being lost because opposition clubs were committed to leagues on Saturdays and friendly Sunday games were generally devalued.

Matters came to a head in 1979 when Maldon was invited to join the Mid-Essex Cricket League. As several of the better clubs on Maldon's fixture list were already committed to the league, the club's management were fearful of missing the opportunity to join them. A decision by the narrowest of majorities was taken by the management committee to accept the invitation, but the decision did not sit happily with the membership and, and for the second time in three years, an extraordinary meeting of the club was requisitioned.

The motion to review the management committee's decision was proposed by Eric Hawkridge and seconded by Bob Harvey (who played with Hawkridge for Gidea Park & Romford before coming to Maldon), Rod Durey, Jim Lionnel, Steve Newman, Nigel Patten and Gary Rayner. The meeting room at the back of the Queen Victoria was packed on the evening of Wednesday, 24 October 1979, when the new Maldon club took the most far reaching decision of its short history.

To the credit of the members present, there was no great debate about the merits of league cricket. The arguments had been exhausted and, like it or not, no club of any standing could remain outside the leagues. The discussion focused on whether the Mid-Essex league was the right one to join, bearing in mind the ambitions some of the leading members held for the future. The meeting overturned the decision of the management committee and decided upon a longer term strategy to secure a place in the Two Counties Championship.

At the time the Essex League, sponsored by Truman's beers, was well established for the top Essex clubs. The majority of these were in London's eastern metropolis, however, and some of the good teams in north Essex had linked with their neighbours in Suffolk to form the Two Counties Championship. Because neither league had a structure that permitted new entrants, it seemed that Maldon's decision had condemned them to a long period in the cricket wilderness. Undaunted, a programme of improvements to the Promenade ground was implemented and, on the advice of league officials, matches against Two Counties clubs were played on a friendly basis.

The break came in 1982 when the Two Counties Championship created a second division to allow in some of the clubs who were serving an apprenticeship similar to Maldon's. Unfortunately, the facilities at the Promenade were considered 'poor compared with others in the competition'. It is easy to sympathise with this judgement when the clubs that were admitted were Abberton and Elmstead Market. It was time for Maldon to play its trump card.

For two years work had been taking place on the development of Drapers Farm. The district council, in full atonement

25. Into the Two Counties Championship 1982. Standing: (left to right) Brian Hunt, Colin Philpott, Eric Hawkridge, Keith Bannister, Malcolm McCleod and Chris Elliott. Sitting: Bob Harvey, Richard Cooper, Peter Manning (captain), Gary Rayner and Glyn Cowlishaw.

for the damage done to cricket by its predecessor, had secured 17 acres of land for sport and recreation as part of the planning permission for housing off Goldhanger Road. Councillors brokered a deal with the cricket and rugby clubs to develop and manage the facilities for their members, in consideration of an initial joint investment of £10,000. It was a perfect opportunity to secure the long-term standing of the new Maldon cricket club.

In 1982, the club assembled a formidable first eleven that beat Abberton, Brightlingsea, Clacton, Dunmow and Harwich from its Two Counties friendly opposition, yet still the application to join the Championship was rejected. Perhaps it was the potential of the new ground that tipped the balance because, after reconsideration, Maldon finally achieved their objective and were accepted as the twelfth club in Division Two of the Two Counties Championship for 1983.

The early season of 1983 was wet. Early games were lost to the weather and it was not until the end of May that Maldon's first Championship game was played at Elmstead Market, where the home team won by six wickets. Unfortunately, Maldon was weakened in its first league season with the departure of two all-rounders, Glyn Cowlishaw and Brian Hunt, who had performed brilliantly in 1982. With those two on board, the team would have looked with confidence at the new challenge, but, without them, the approach was more tentative.

Chris Elliott carried heavy responsibility to score runs with the more ephemeral support of Malcolm McCleod and Keith Bannister, while Colin Philpott advanced his reputation for reliability. The bowling relied on Cooper, Hawkridge and skipper, Manning, in the seam department with Bob Barnes, promoted to the first eleven, proving the success story of the season with his off breaks. A healthy squad of able youngsters included Gary Rayner, Daf Newton, Kevin Shoemake, Ian Hastings, Brian Corderoy and Ian Binns, while Bob Harvey kept wicket, sometimes brilliantly.

By the end of June, the only victory had been against Dunmow. Rayner took six wickets for 52 runs and in the chase was led by Elliott (82) and Philpott (66 not out). Then, in a remarkable demonstration of growing confidence, eight wins were recorded from nine matches during July and August.

Matches were 45 overs a side and the average total score for a team was around 150 runs. Elliott's purple patch that earned him 300 runs in five matches was the most tangible contribution to the sequence of wins but there were many other important individual performances. Bill Greenwood, veteran of the powerful Chelmsford team of the 1940s, was even pressed into action against Ipswich & East Suffolk and took six wickets for 32 runs. Late runs by Corderoy and wickets by Barnes in the last game of the season gave Maldon victory over a Braintree side that included Nick King, Keith Merrell and Mick Rust, all of whom would become Maldon players in later years.

In its first season Maldon finished third in Division Two of the Two Counties Championship, behind Dunmow and Abberton, both of whom it had beaten during the year. Had the confidence that developed during the second half of the season been discovered earlier, the club could well have achieved promotion to Division One at the first attempt. As it turned out, Maldon were to finish in third position on two further occasions before they secured second place – and promotion – in 1988.

Chapter 33
Reputation restored

The new Maldon club quickly settled to the standard of cricket enjoyed by the Two Counties Championship and began to rebuild the reputation among top clubs that had been enjoyed 100 years before. In 1985, two of the founder members of the new club, Sue and Peter Manning, stood down from their positions of president and first eleven captain, to be replaced by John House and Eric Hawkridge. During the next five years the strength and standing of the club developed at a tremendous pace.

It was a time of great enthusiasm for cricket, with sometimes as many as five teams in action on a Saturday and Sunday, as well as a regular Wednesday eleven. The development of the new ground at Drapers Farm gave the hard-working core of club members a clear objective and the influx of new players assured the growing strength of teams on the field. A revitalised cricket festival week was launched at Drapers Farm in 1985 with the aim of raising the club's profile in the town and in wider cricket circles.

Within a couple of years the cricket festival was established as the annual showcase for the club, attracting fine players and key figures from Essex and Suffolk cricket. President, John House, was instrumental to this success, introducing numerous influential colleagues into Maldon cricket and making Drapers Farm a popular watering hole for off-duty professional cricketers. The club established profitable relations with local firms through festival sponsorship and will forever be indebted to the generosity of two club members, John Hill and Doug Golding for their support at this important stage of the club's growth.

26. Promotion in the Two Counties Championship 1988. Standing: (left to right) Paul Vickers, Pat Noonan, Mark Chapman, Mark Hawkes, Nick King and Nigel Hinton. Sitting: Martin White, Brian Corderoy, Mick Brown (captain), Chris Elliott and Mick Springett.

By 1988 the stage was set for a new and bright chapter in the history of the Maldon club. Links with the Essex county club had elevated Drapers Farm to a venue for Second Eleven cricket and both future England captain, Nasser Hussain, and international fast bowler, Neil Foster, made appearances there. Future Essex captain, Paul Prichard, became a good friend (and later vice-president) of the club and, with his assistance, two young professional bowlers, David Boden and Nick Derbyshire, came to play their club cricket at Maldon in the early 1990s.

Mick Brown became first eleven captain in 1988 with Nick King, a coach at the Essex county cricket school, as his deputy. Maldon played their first season in the top division of the Two Counties Championship, finishing fifth out of 14 clubs, thanks to the runs of Brown and Chris Elliott and the all round contribution of the Australian, Mark Chapman. Prospects were looking even healthier on the youth front with young teenagers Ian Elliott, Rob Barber, Peter Wargent, Jeff Cook, Marc Gozzett, Martin White and Paul Raymond all starting to break into first eleven cricket.

During the ten years of his leadership, Brown helped to nurture the talents of these young cricketers, most of whom would form the nucleus of the side that eventually forced its way into the East Anglian Premier League in 2001. In the early years, however, much was owed to the enthusiasm and persistence of Brown in consistently achieving performances that kept Maldon in the top six clubs in the Championship table.

As Elliott and Barber began to shine as the best opening partnership in the league, Brown was able to take a more relaxed approach to his own performance. However, his personal contribution to the success of the club on the field was enormous: in 14 years he compiled more than 8600 runs at an average of 32, mostly in the Two Counties Championship and often in difficult situations. Occasionally he was tempted to employ his off spin, especially after he captured the wicket of Graham Gooch in Paul Prichard's benefit match at Drapers Farm in 1996.

Maldon also hosted a benefit day for Neil Foster in 1993, when he retired from first-class cricket after 174 matches for Essex and 28 for England. His career was regrettably interrupted by injury and it was during a return to fitness that he first played at Drapers Farm in 1988. Later he became coach at Maldon, helping the team to secure runner-up position in the East Anglian Premier League in 2003.

As well as Gooch and Foster, other internationals on show at Drapers Farm for the benefit matches were John Childs, Nasser Hussain, Mark Ilott, Ronnie Irani, John Lever, Derek Pringle, John Stephenson and Salim Malik, who was later discredited by match fixing allegations. Although Prichard did not play international cricket, he scored prolifically for Essex, including 245 against Leicestershire in 1990 in a second wicket record partnership of 405 with Graham Gooch. Prichard too, had injury problems, and played several games

27. Powerhouse president. John House did much to return the club to the top during his eleven years as president between 1985 and 1996.

for Maldon when returning to fitness and, in 1995, became a vice-president of the club. In 1988, he took over the captaincy of Essex when Graham Gooch retired.

During the 11 years that John House was president, the new Maldon club made an indelible mark in the world of club

28. Friends and leaders. Mick Brown with Paul Prichard before the benefit match against Essex in 1996.

cricket. His influence established Drapers Farm as a favourite port of call for many first-class cricketers resting from their day's exertions at Chelmsford and brought young professionals into the club's playing ranks. His contacts with the Waverley club in Sydney brought over a succession of talented young Australians to cement Maldon's standing in the Two Counties Championship.

Mick Brown provided the perfect partner on the playing side and the support of the large core of progressive club officials enabled the most ambitious projects to be achieved. It was as though the club had reached the twentieth century pinnacle of the same history that had earned visits from Grace, Hornby and Spofforth in the 1870s.

The only ambition not achieved was to be Two Counties division one champions. On the contrary, it was a cruel twist of fate that brought relegation from division one in the final year of Brown's captaincy in 1998. But the shock waves that resulted destroyed the creeping complacency in the club and again created the positive energy needed to scale even greater heights.

Chapter 34

The Waverley connection

One important factor of Maldon's success on the field from the 1980s was the contribution of young Australian players from Waverley Cricket Club. Now renamed 'Easts' to represent the eastern suburbs of Sydney, the Waverley ground is a steep climb up the hill from the tourist paradise of Bondi Beach. The Australian connection grew from a friendship between John House, who became Maldon's president in 1985, and Bob Horsell, the Waverley president whose 6300 runs in his playing days between 1963 and 1988, earned him a place among the top ten run scorers in Waverley's history.

During the 100 years of its history, Waverley, founded in 1894, found a place among the leading clubs in the tough Sydney grade competition. Cricketing legends like Jack Gregory, Alan Kippax and Jack Fingleton played for the club while, in more modern times, overseas players of the calibre of Tony Greig, Geoffrey Boycott and Malcolm Marshall have all spent seasons there. Bruce Francis, who came to Essex as an opening batsman in the early 1970s and went on to represent Australia, was a Waverley man and Paul Prichard, destined for the Essex captaincy, spent his early winters on the tough Sydney circuit. Prichard later played for Maldon while recovering from injury and became a vice-president of the club, together with Waverley president, Bob Horsell, in 1995.

When Maldon won promotion to join the top clubs in 1988, outspoken skipper, Mick Brown, gave notice to a packed but unconvinced annual dinner of the Two Counties Championship that, 'Maldon is here to stay'. If he was not to eat his words, Brown knew that the team needed extra strength to help mould the clutch of talented youngsters who were coming

29. Waverley and Maldon players take on Essex in 1996. Standing: (left to right) Ben Day, Robbie Barber, Peter Wargent, Jeff Cook, Mike Benicos and Mike McLellan. Kneeling: Neale Harrington, Ian Elliott, Mick Brown, Marc Gozzett and David Hunter.

through. Thus began the tradition of young Sydneysiders spending English summers coaching youngsters, experiencing the English game and unfailingly enjoying themselves.

The first visitor in 1988, slow left arm bowler, Mark Chapman, although recruited through Waverley, played for Sutherland. He scored 1350 runs for Maldon at an average of 50 and, though his bowling was less effective on stodgy English pitches, he still took 79 wickets for less than 20 apiece.

Between 1989 and 1998, Waverley players made around 13,000 runs for Maldon at an average of nearly 50. Although the majority were specialist batsmen, between them they took almost 200 wickets at around 20 runs apiece. Their performances were a crucial factor in Maldon's continuing success on the field, but their influence went deeper still. Each player brought his own brand of rugged self-belief, resourcefulness and refusal to accept defeat – traits that typify Australian sportsmen. These attributes rubbed off onto the young home grown players at the club, some of whom, like Ian Elliott, Paul Raymond and Peter Wargent, made exchange visits to play at Waverley during the English winter.

The young Australians brought discipline to their coaching but, for the majority of youngsters not destined to shine at the game, they also brought a sense of fun and enjoyment. For spectators they expressed high talent on the field of play, with many vintage performances, and were always ready with relaxed and friendly company off it. In short, they brought a fresh dimension to Maldon that could not fail to improve the good health of its cricket.

Waverley could have had no better ambassador than Geoff Nixon who came in 1989 and scored 1865 runs, more than any other overseas player since. President's son, Mike Horsell, did manage to score more runs because he liked Maldon so much he came for two seasons in 1992 and 1995. In those two years he made 2715 runs and took 74 wickets – and performed enthusiastically behind the stumps as well.

Wicket-keeping was the speciality of David Hunter who spent the summer of 1997 at Maldon. He was immaculate behind the stumps and his batting was often heroic as he compiled 861 league runs at an average of 57. Classical batsmen, Darren Kingdon, who later forced his way into the Queensland state side after moving north from Sydney, came in 1991 and Mike Benicos was the visitor in 1996. Both scored heavily finishing their seasons with an average of over 50 runs per innings.

Paul Pratt (1993) and Kevin Roche (1994) came primarily as bowlers but each scored over 1000 runs. Pratt took 39 wickets with his right arm off-spin, but Roche was disappointingly injured after taking 20 wickets early in the season and was unable to show off the best of his right arm fast bowling. He concentrated instead on scoring runs and compiled a total of 1356, more than any other player that year, at an average of

48 per innings. Married and living in London, he made a rare return to Maldon in 2000 to appear in a league play-off match.

As if to demonstrate the key role of their overseas players, in 1990, when arrangements to secure one fell through, Maldon slipped to their lowest ever position in the Two Counties Championship. That is until the disastrous season of 1998 when the club was relegated back into the second division, despite 1200 runs and 37 wickets from Mike McLellan, the Waverley player who joined the club that year.

When John House moved from Maldon and ended his stint as president in 1996, the Waverley connection was maintained by Chris Elliott. The knowledge of Bob Horsell and contact with the players who had spent seasons at Maldon helped to keep the club supplied with cricketers from different parts of Australia to meet the stringent challenges of premier league cricket.

Chapter 35

East Anglian Premier League

When the fates conspire against a team it is doomed. There is no simple explanation for the Maldon club's miserable performance in the Two Counties Championship in 1998, when repeated defeats left it languishing at the bottom of the table. But the shock waves of relegation provided the spur that was needed to dispel the air of complacency and impel the club towards the East Anglian Premier League in 2001.

There was no hint of the traumas to come in 1997. Ian Elliott and Rob Barber scored their accustomed weight of runs and the Australian, David Hunter, contributed magnificently with the bat and behind the stumps. The team finished fourth out of 14 in the league and brought the first silverware to Drapers Farm by winning the League Cup. The 1998 season promised continued success with the same core of players with all rounder, Mike McLellan, replacing Hunter as the overseas player.

Elliott scored 738 league runs at an average of 43, but received little consistent support from others. Match after match slipped from Maldon's grasp as they lost 12 of the 17 games played and finished in the second relegation position, just above old rivals, Braintree. Mick Brown, in his last year as captain, found the season's performance 'a bitter pill to swallow' but could offer no simple diagnosis for the team's failure. The answer lay in the mental approach which seemed to lack the consistent toughness and focus needed to win in top level sport.

Rob Barber took over the captain's mantle in 1999 and the winning habit quickly returned to the team in the lower division. Elliott and Barber each scored over a thousand runs and the middle-order scored fluently when required. Paul Raymond and Neale Harrington were the leading wicket takers, although Elliott and Barber performed well in this department also, taking 50 wickets between them. Maldon achieved the sought after promotion, finishing second in the table, this time behind old rivals, Braintree.

When Maldon returned to division one in 2000, the league had been restructured in consequence of the creation of the East Anglian Premier League. Bury St Edmunds, Clacton, Halstead and Mildenhall had all been elevated to the higher level, leaving a slimmed down Two Counties Championship with just ten clubs in each division. Without the stronger clubs to contend with, Maldon swept all before it, winning 13 of 15 matches and taking the Two Counties Championship for the first time.

The triumph was achieved with the same core of youthful players who had lost heart two years before. Now two years older and mentally stronger they showed what they could do. The performance was even more remarkable because injuries to Elliott and Barber dried up the team's usual fountainhead of runs. Peter Wargent, who had been remodelled by a winter in Australia, stepped into the breach, scoring 794 runs at an average of 57, and young David Randall, in his first full season with the senior side, made nearly 400 runs at an average of 40. Jeff Cook, completing his transformation from bowler to batsman, contributed 337 runs at an average of 34.

The key to Maldon's success was, however, the ability to bowl sides out. Since the days of Andy Donner and Derek Brewer the team had struggled to find match winning bowlers but, in 2000, the services of Australian, Jay Trevaskis were secured. Trevaskis, who played Sydney grade cricket for Manley, had come to England to play in Cornwall, where Chris Elliott's extensive network of contacts reported him to be less than happy. As Maldon specialised in dispensing happiness to their overseas players, Trevaskis was persuaded to join the club.

He was not a star performer for Manley but his gifts of hard work and commitment, harnessed to brisk and straight bowling, were the ingredient Maldon needed. As the season progressed, his unquenchable enthusiasm for victims increased and he finished with a tally of 55 wickets (out of 130 taken by all bowlers) at an average of under 16 apiece. Maldon had earned a chance to rejoin the big clubs in the East Anglian Premier League, a chance they took by beating Cambridgeshire champions, Long Stanton, in a play-off match.

The East Anglian Premier League was created by the England Cricket Board in 1999 as part of the initiative to breathe new life into the national game. It was part of an overall move to create a unified structure containing international cricket and its grass roots origins in the recreational game. Premier leagues were set up across the country to form a bridge that enabled talented amateur cricketers to make the transition from club to first-class cricket. The East Anglian Premier League brought together the best clubs in Cambridgeshire, Norfolk, Suffolk and north Essex.

Maldon's problems on the field in 2001 were more about coping with ex-professionals and top class overseas players than with young home-grown opponents. The subtleties of the longer form of the game and a complicated points system took some time to learn as the team struggled to come to terms with a much higher standard of cricket. The limited overs format of the Two Counties Championship was replaced by a game that reintroduced declarations, drawn matches and the need to bowl out the opposition to win. Above all the new league demanded the ability to focus for 120 overs, any mental weaknesses being punished without compunction.

The season became a lesson in gathering points, clinging on to hard fought draws, battling for every wicket and eking out every possible run in defeat. One win did come against Cambridge Granta at Drapers Farm and the team managed to stave off relegation, thanks to the luckless Halstead who finished bottom after a disastrous season. Although perform-

30. Runners up in the East Anglian Premier League 2003. Standing: (left to right) Tim Bondin, Glen Batticciotto, Alastair Cook, Colin Barry, David Randall and Adrian McCoubrey. Sitting: Paul Symons, Ian Elliott, Jeff Cook (captain), Robbie Barber, Jimmy Ainscough and Peter Wargent.

ance was disappointing, team morale was high. Colin Barry from Wests club in Sydney led the bowling attack with pace and class, while Elliott and Wargent each scored nearly 500 runs at averages of well over 40.

The lessons were well learned in the first season of premier league cricket. In 2002, Jeff Cook took over the captaincy from Rob Barber and the club finished more comfortably in the bottom half of the table with three wins. Jimmy Ainscough joined the team as a wicketkeeper/batsman and the classy young Alastair Cook began to contribute significantly when home from Bedford School. When the team was reinforced by the return of Australian, Colin Barry, by Essex fringe player, Adrian McCoubrey, and Australian under-19 player, Glen Batticciotto, in 2003, it was catapulted up the league to finish in runner-up position. Cook's century against Cambridge Granta at Drapers Farm, watched by Keith Fletcher, took him into the Essex county team by the end of the season.

Maldon had not seen itself as a premier league club and

made no move to join when the proposals first emerged. The success and enthusiasm that followed the shame of relegation in 1998 swept the team into the top level and an influx of powerful players secured its place among the top two clubs by 2003. But the strength of the league continued to escalate under the influence of powerful sponsors and patrons who imported two test match players, West Indian Stuart Williams, and New Zealander, Ian Sinclair to the circuit in 2004. Maldon, stripped of most of its own top talent, once more struggled with the problems of relegation.

Chapter 36
Yesterday and tomorrow

If the purpose of history is to inform the present, then this excursion into the past may be more than an exercise in nostalgia. When cricket was first played in Maldon more than 250 years ago, the gentlemen merchants were following the fashion of the time. Winning mattered to them, both for the satisfaction of victory itself and for the money that accrued in an era of manic gambling. Thus the early Maldon cricket promoters combed the Dengie Hundred for the best players, sometimes using their business contacts to import men from further afield. At the same time they took steps to ensure their opponents employed only local players.

As the years passed and round arm bowling made cricket a more dangerous game, the rough saltings at Potman Marsh no longer provided a suitable surface on which to play. The accession of Queen Victoria ushered in an honourable phase of the game after match fixing scandals had corrupted earlier years. The ethos of the public school prevailed and the analogy of the 'straight bat' to signify fair play upon life's green playing fields was born. The reality, of course, was rather different with keen brained professionals keeping gamesmanship alive, and the Lords committee continuing to rely on grazing sheep – rather than new fangled mowers – to prepare their pitches.

At Maldon, however, it is difficult to see how the cricket club could have prospered in an era of country house cricket without the move to the Fairfield. The fashionable clubs, notably Colchester, Chelmsford and Witham began to prepare better grounds using the newly invented cylinder mowers, pioneered by Ransomes of Ipswich, and the heavy rollers that came in increased numbers from iron founders. Those clubs were also increasingly dominated by the sons of the great and the good of the county, after their passage through public school and university. In the mid-nineteenth century, the Maldon club, using the new ground technology, produced facilities to compare with any in the county. Although not blessed with the sons of the upper classes, Maldon's backers held sufficient sway to maintain the best fixtures and the organizers knew how to get strong teams onto the park.

The significant point is that the cricket club was part of the town's establishment. In the early days, cricket clubs were formed by the patrons who put up the money, mostly as inducements to recruit good players. Those who financed the club – the members – had power of decision in all matters, including who played and who did not. The players were not expected to contribute, unless they were themselves patrons whose motivation was to play the game. Maldon were never in that class, but nor was the cricket club expected to be self-financing. The management committee in Victorian times was large, including names of prominent citizens who never appeared in match reports and who, doubtless, assisted with the expenses of the ground and the employment of professionals like Frank Silcock.

It is significant that the initiative for the All England Eleven match in 1873 came from Humpherys and Sprague, two merchants and pillars of the corporation, whose fellow town traders were to make up the subscription list for the match expenses. Tomlinson, Self and Timperley, key playing members of the cricket club, were all elected to the corporation but were small fry compared with others whose civic duties extended to the committee of the cricket club. It may be significant that when the corporation became increasingly discredited by economic downturn, internal bickering, debt and financial irregularities, the cricket club too started on a downward course.

Tomlinson, the man behind the rise to prominence, perhaps held onto the reins too long and was an old man when he finally ceded the captaincy around 1890. By then the club was headed towards the rocks, losing credibility with fashionable opponents, failing to rebuild team strength and unable to replace the strong organization that had taken it to the top. For 20 years it struggled along, disappearing from sight around 1910 and losing the Fairfield ground that had been taken by the new grammar school.

When the Town club reformed in the 1920s it was an independent group of cricketers, largely unconnected with Maldon's wider affairs. Similarly, when the Strollers and Old Maldonians clubs came into existence later, their focus was simply on playing weekend cricket. The days when cricket and civic business had gone hand in hand were long gone, to the extent that their interests were now polarised. The council fell down badly on their responsibilities for recreation to the point where the Strollers, more accepting of their lot than most clubs, threatened to abandon the Promenade ground because of its poor condition. Meanwhile the luckless Town club were obliged to abandon their part of the Promenade to allow a bowling green and tennis courts to be built. Old Maldonians in their turn became homeless, having reoccupied the Fairfield for a few years while relations with the fading grammar school were good.

For those readers whose memories stretch back to the formation of the new Maldon club in 1976, the lessons of history are probably all too clear. For the younger generation, poised to take responsibility for the future of Maldon cricket, here are some conclusions spelled out. A strong cricket club needs high quality facilities and good management. Its organization needs new faces replacing the old so that new enthusiasm keeps a forward looking, rather than a backward looking, ethos within the club.

An existence separate from the life of the town is a lonely one. Good relations with civic and business organizations does not just demonstrate maturity and respect, it brings tangible benefits. Public money is not spent on introspective organizations and private money, in the form of donations and sponsorship, is essential to meet the running costs of a top club.

And Maldon is a top club again, sitting within reach of the first-class game. In the same way that a century and a half ago professionals were needed to maintain that status, so today, in the East Anglian Premier League, players of exceptional talent have to be recruited to reach the standards being set by the more wealthy clubs.

Bibliography

The main sources of information on matches and players

ACS (1987) *Essex cricketers 1876–1986*, Nottingham: Association of Cricket Statisticians

Bailey, Philip, Philip Thorn and Peter Wynne-Thomas (1993) *Who's who of cricketers*, London: Hamlyn, second edition

Buckley, G. B. (1935) *Fresh light on 18th century cricket: a collection of 1000 new cricket notices from 1697–1800* AD, Birmingham: Cotterell and Sons

Buckley, G. B. (1937) *Fresh light on pre-Victorian cricket: 1709–1837*, Birmingham: Cotterell and Sons

Chelmsford (later *Essex*) *Chronicle*, 1764–1955

Cricket Scores and Biographies compiled variously by Haygarth, Lillywhite and the MCC and republished by Roger Heavens 1996–2003

Dowsett, Michael (1955) *The day of 'the demon'*, published by the author, reprinted 2002

Goulstone, J. (1993) *Early club and village cricket*, published by the author (available from Essex Library Collection AA 796.358)

Lemmon, David and Michael Marshall (1987) *Essex CCC: the offical history*, n.p.: Red Rose Cricket Books

Maldon Cricket Club Handbooks 1980–2003, published by the club

Other sources used

Bury & Norwich Post

Essex Weekly News

Ipswich Journal

Maldon Advertiser

Maldon Express

Maldon & Burnham Standard

Meredith, Anthony (1987) *The demon and the lobster: Charles Kortright and Digby Jephson, remarkable bowlers in the golden age*, Erith: Kingswood Press

Morning Herald

Morrison, J. (1994) *Up the waves: a history of the Waverley Cricket Club Inc. 1894–1994*, Waverley Cricket Club

Southend Standard

Williams, E. M. (1951) *Cricket, let's look at the past*, Maldon Cricket Club

Williams, E. M. (1955) *Cricket: a bicentenary in an Essex setting*, published by the author

Wynne-Thomas, Peter (1992) *The official history of Nottinghamshire County Cricket Club*, with a personal view by Derek Randall, Helm Series

For background on Essex and Maldon local history

Brown, A. F. J. (1969) *Essex at work 1700–1815*, Chelmsford: Essex County Council

Brown, A. F. J. (1972) *Essex people 1750–1900: from their diaries, memoirs and letters*, Chelmsford: Essex County Council

Brown, A. F. J. (1996) *Prosperity and poverty: rural Essex 1700–1815*, Essex Record Office Publications

Grace, D. R. and D. C. Phillips (1975) *Ransomes of Ipswich: a history of the firm and a guide to its records*, Institute of Agricultural History

Hughes, David (1996) *The Maldonians: voices of Maldon 1872–1914*, Maldon: The Folk Corporation

Hussey, Stephen and Laura Swash (1994) *Horrid Lights: 19th Century Incediarism in Essex*, Centre for Local History Publications, No. 5, University of Essex

Kemp, Peter (1955) *The Bentall story: commemorating 150 years service to agriculture*, Maldon: E. & H. Bentall

Kemp, P. K. (1964) *The continuing years: a short historical account of the development and growth of the family firm of Sadds*, Maldon: John Sadd and Son

Petchey, W. J. (1991) *A prospect of Maldon: 1500-1689*, Essex Record Office Publications

Smith, J. R. (1981) *The Borough of Maldon: 1688-1768*, thesis by the author in Essex Record Office

Smith, M. L. (1980/81) 'The Maldon–Braintree railway', *Essex Journals*, Essex Archaeological and Historical Congress

Stubbings, Ken (1988) *Here's good luck to the pint pot*, Kelvin Brown Publications

Thompson, J. O. (1933) *Dr Salter of Tolleshunt D'Arcy in the County of Essex*, Essex Library Collection 006687156

For background to early cricket

Altham, H. S. and E. W. Swanton (1948) *History of cricket*, with an introduction by Sir Pelham Warner, London: Allen and Unwin

Arlott, John (ed.) (1948) *From Hambledon to Lords: the classics of cricket*, London: Christopher Johnson Publisher

Arlott, John (1949) *The middle ages of cricket*, London: Christopher Johnson Publisher

Barrett, Norman (1994) *Daily Telegraph chronicle of cricket*, Enfield: Guinness Publishing Limited

Barty-King, Hugh (1979) *Quilt winders and pod shavers: the history of cricket bat and ball manufacture*, London: MacDonald and Jane's

Birley, Derek (1999) *A social history of English cricket*, London: Aurum Press

Brodribb, Gerald (1962) *Felix on the bat: being a memoir of Nicholas Felix*, London: n.p.

Brodribb, Gerald (2002) *Felix and the eleven of England*, Manchester: Boundary Books

Brooke, Robert (1991) *A history of the county cricket championship*, Newton Abbott: Gullane Children's Books

Brookes, Christopher (1978) *English cricket: the game and its players through the ages*, London: Weidenfeld and Nicolson

Caffyn, William (1899) *Seventy-one not out: the reminiscences*, edited by 'Mid-On' (R. P. Daft), Edinburgh: Blackwood

Daft, Richard (1893) *Kings of cricket: reminiscences and anecdotes with hints on the game*, Bristol: n.p.

Eagar, Patrick (1992) *Caught in the frame: 150 years of cricket photography*, London: Collins Willow

Evans, R. D. C. (1988) *Cricket grounds: the evolution, maintenance and construction of natural turf cricket tables and outfields*, Bingley: The Sports Turf Research Institute

Lemmon, David (1993) *For the love of the game: an oral history of first-class cricket*, London: Michael Joseph Publishers.

Lillywhite, Fred (1980) *The English cricketers trip to Canada and the United States in 1859*, London: Worlds Work Limited

March, Russell (1982) *The cricketers of Vanity Fair*, Exeter: Webb & Bower

Marlar, Robin (1979) *The story of cricket*, London: Marshall Cavendish

Marshall, John (1961) *The duke who was cricket*, London: Frederick Miller Limited

Midwinter, Eric (1992) *Illustrated history of county cricket*, London: Kingswood

Morrah, Patrick (1986) *Alfred Mynn and the cricketers of his time*, London: Constable

Mote, Ashley (ed.) (1998) *John Nyren's cricketers of my time, the original version*, London: Robson Books Limited

Mote, Ashley (1999) *The glory days of cricket*, London: Robson Books Limited

Pycroft, Revd James (1862) *The cricket field: or the history and science of the game of cricket*, London: Longman Green and Roberts, fourth edition

Pycroft, Revd James (1865) *Cricketana*, London: Longman Green and Roberts

Rait Kerr, R. S. (1950) *The laws of cricket: their history and growth*, London: Longmans, Green and Company Limited

The Times (1937) *MCC 1787–1937*, London: The Times Publishing Company

Underdown, David (2001) *Start of play: cricket and culture in 18th-century England*, Harmondsworth: Penguin Books

Waghorn, H. T. (1906) *The dawn of cricket*, MCC

Williams, Marcus and Gordon Phillips (1990) *The Wisden book of cricket memorabilia*, Oxford: Lennard Publishing

Wynne-Thomas, Peter (1989) *The complete history of cricket tours at home and abroad*, London: Hamlyn

Index